BEGIN FISHING
THE RIGHT WAY

Ian Ball

RIGHT WAY

CONTENTS

1
INTRODUCTION

The thrill of catching a powerful fish on rod and line is an experience you'll always treasure.

Freshwater fishing and sea fishing are grand sports and healthy recreations that introduce us to the splendours of Nature's magnificent world of colour and beauty.

The first part of "Begin Fishing The Right Way" explores *freshwater fishing*. The second part, commencing with Chapter 17 on page 89, examines *sea fishing*.

To achieve a high degree of angling success, we must understand the correct tackle, best baits and methods to use, and the right places to fish.

This book takes us on a guided tour of freshwater and sea fishing locations; shows the great spots to fish; gives valuable success hints, tackle notes and tips; suggests fascinating activities to develop and sharpen our angling skills, and points out some of the remarkable water creatures and plants to watch for.

Observant anglers can become expert naturalists. All anglers are keen to conserve the host of impressive and interesting species of water life: plants, birds, animals, insects, fish etc., whose company we share while fishing from the water's edge.

You may be a beginner angler as you start reading this book, but after you finish, you'll know more about fishing than many experts.

2
FRESHWATER FISHING

Freshwater fishing is the sporting pursuit with rod and line of fishes that live in fresh water: still or flowing water, which is more-or-less drinkable, not salt water.

Tackle dealers

Get to know your local specialist tackle dealer; visit the shop and have a good look round. Chat, ask for advice and guidance on all fishing matters. Your friendly tackle dealer will help select the right tackle; provide the correct freshwater *rod licence* – essential to fish legally, and recommend waters worth fishing. Your tackle dealer can also supply any *fishing permit* required in addition to the rod licence, to fish a particularly worthwhile water.

Support the tackle dealer with *your* valued custom, and you'll be rewarded handsomely with the dealer's expert hints, tips and details of the latest tackle developments and "secret" fishing hotspots.

Close seasons

Nearly all freshwater fish are classified as "coarse fish". Trout and salmon are classed as "game fish". In most parts of England and Wales no fishing is allowed for *coarse fish* between March 15th and June 15th inclusive (their breeding season). The close season for *brown trout* is from 1st October to the last day of February, inclusive. The close season for *salmon* is November 1st to January 31st inclusive.

Scotland, Northern Ireland and Eire, each have different arrangements, which may vary from one water to another. Check with the respective Tourist Boards, or local tackle dealers, for up-to-date details.

Outwit the fish

To catch fish think one step ahead. Big fish stay unhooked

because foolish anglers can't outwit them. Let Nature remind you how to hunt – be animal cunning from the start. Wear drab-colour clothes that blend with the background; wear nothing bright or flashy. Put tackle together away from the waterside and approach quietly; tread softly. Creep from one bank edge hiding-place to another (bush, tree etc). Scan the water for promising spots to fish. Be aware that alert fishes can see images of natural food and anglers' baits reflected downwards from the surface of *calm water* (which acts as a mirror) and can at the same time, watch the bankside for motion betraying the presence of prowling anglers.

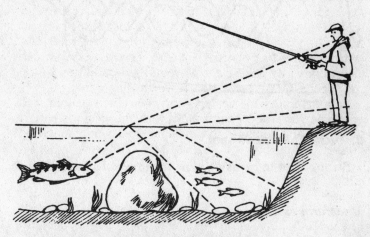

1. Fish's eye view of water and bankside.

Never feel self-conscious about crouching or crawling towards open bankside areas devoid of cover. Nobody will think you silly when you land the BIG fish others can't catch!

Relax to succeed
This book tells all you need know to locate the right spots to fish, and the best ways to present tempting hookbait. The rest is up to you. When you're certain you've found a stretch of water that holds fish, apply the knowledge you've learned and fish your way to success. Relax, be confident you know

enough to hook that Big one... And when it seizes your hookbait, don't panic. Remain calm and in control. Reel-in line, and land your fish.

Practical skills
Enthusiasm alone won't catch fish. You must learn the basic skills of knot-tying and casting.

Tucked half blood knot

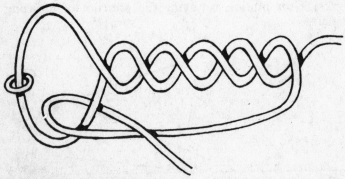

2. Tucked half blood knot.

Strong knot to tie fishing line to the eye of a hook, swivel etc.

Underarm cast

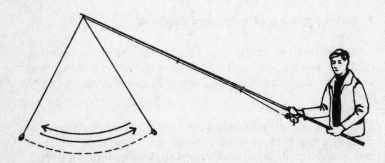

3. Underarm cast.

The underarm style does not cast a long way, but is accurate and adequate for close-range fishing, and perfect for casting in a restricted space. Swing the line with a pendulum action; release line from reel on the upswing. Stop reel when your hookbait has entered the water.

Overhead cast

4. Overhead cast.

The overhead style casts line a long distance. First, see you're not hemmed in by line-snagging tree branches or bushes. Look towards the spot you want to reach with your cast; bring the rod slowly up over your shoulder, then speed the overhead sweep and release line when your rod is pointing in the direction of your target area. Hold rod steady until hookbait enters the water, then stop reel.

3
FISH

Soft-finned fish

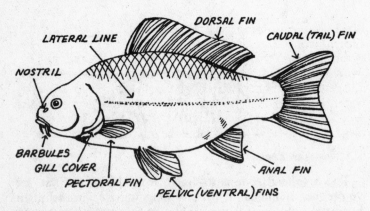

NOSTRIL

LATERAL LINE

DORSAL FIN

CAUDAL (TAIL) FIN

BARBULES

GILL COVER

PECTORAL FIN

PELVIC (VENTRAL) FINS

ANAL FIN

5. General features of soft-finned fish.

The *dorsal* and *anal* fins enable the fish to balance; the *pectoral* and *pelvic* fins assist the fish's movements, and the *caudal* fin, combined with body movement, propels the fish through water. Some species of fish have sensitive *barbules* to feel and taste for food hidden from the fish's sight, at the water bottom. The *lateral line* is a series of scales with tiny holes, giving the appearance of a line. The "holes" are pores through which changes in pressure are communicated to the fish's brain. The lateral line of pores warns the fish of approaching objects; lurking predators, and hidden prey.

    Spiny-finned fish, like perch and zander, have a spiny dorsal fin and a second, *posterior dorsal* fin on the back, close behind.

Barbel (*Barbus barbus*).
Classification: Coarse fish.

Natural home: Rivers and streams.
Popular angling methods: Float fishing; legering.

TIPS
Barbel like fast flowing and deep water, especially over a gravel bottom. Fish for barbel near weed beds; underwater holes, hollows; bankside undercuts; weir-pools; eddies, and beneath bridges. Present your hookbait on, or near, the water bottom.

Bleak *(Alburnus alburnus)*.
Classification: Coarse fish.
Natural home: Rivers; some lakes in England and Wales.
Notes: Bleak are small fish; seldom exceed 175mm in length, and not often deliberately fished for. Bleak like slow flowing water, and feed near the surface. They were once popular as food, and netted in large numbers. In the nineteenth century, bleak's shiny scales were used in the manufacture of artificial pearls!

Bronze Bream *(Abramis brama)*.
Classification: Coarse fish.
Natural home: Rivers, lakes, ponds; also stocked in canals, pits and reservoirs.
Popular angling methods: Legering; float fishing; spinning.

TIPS
Bream like slow flowing and still waters. Fish for bream on, or near, the water bottom – in deep water well away from the bank.

Common Carp *(Cyprinus carpio)*.
Classification: Coarse fish.
Natural home: Lakes, ponds, rivers; also stocked in pits, reservoirs and some canals.
Popular angling methods: Legering; float fishing; free-lining.

TIPS
Carp thrive in the warm and heavily weeded stillwaters, and

slow-flowing rivers of central and southern England. Fish for carp on, or near, the water bottom; beside water plants, and between weed beds.

Carp like deep, shaded water during daytime, and stay away from the bankside on noisy, well-fished waters until dusk or after dark, when they move into weedy and reedy shallows to feed.

Chub *(Leuciscus cephalus).*
Classification: Coarse fish.
Natural home: Slow rivers and fast flowing streams; also stocked in some ponds and pits. Found mainly in England, parts of Wales and southern Scotland.
Popular angling methods: Legering; float fishing; free-lining; spinning; fly fishing.

TIPS
Chub feed at any depth, from water bottom to surface. Fish for chub in shaded water below overhanging waterside shrubs and trees. Chub are fond of hiding in underwater holes, hollows and bankside undercuts. They also hide in ambush near weed beds, eddies; beneath bridges; at the mouth of inflowing streams, and behind submerged obstacles: fallen trees, tree roots, boulders etc.

Dace *(Leuciscus leuciscus).*
Classification: Coarse fish.
Natural home: Fast and medium-fast flowing rivers and streams in England and Wales.
Popular angling methods: Float fishing; free-lining; legering; fly fishing.

TIPS
Dace are small, energetic shoal fish, and rarely grow more than 250mm in length. Dace love fast, streamy runs of water between weed beds. In warm weather, fish for dace at, or near, the water surface; on hot days, dace shoals feed at mid-water depth; during cold, wintry weather, dace search the water bottom for food.

Eel *(Anguilla anguilla).*
Classification: Coarse fish.
Natural home: Eels feel at home in still or flowing freshwater in most parts of Britain and Eire.
Popular angling methods: Legering; free-lining.

TIPS
Eels feed enthusiastically along the water bottom, at dusk and after dark in warm weather; right through the night in summer! Eels live in bankside holes; amongst sunken debris, and thick weed. Eels hunt by scent, so present a "smelly" hookbait (fresh dead fish – strips, chunks or whole; earthworm; cheese etc.) in a promising spot, and wait for the eels to track their way to you. Land the eel as fast as possible after hooking, or it wraps around an underwater obstacle and snags and snaps your line!

Grayling *(Thymallus thymallus).*
Classification: Member of the Salmon family (Salmonidae) of "game" fish, but grayling breed the same time as coarse fish, so are classed as *coarse* fish.
Natural home: Fast flowing rivers and streams, where well-oxygenated, clear water runs over a gravel or chalk bed.
Popular angling methods: Float fishing; fly fishing; free-lining; legering.

TIPS
Grayling can be caught at any depth, though prefer feeding at mid-water depth, and on the water bottom. Present your hookbait in fast, streamy runs; near weed beds, bank undercuts, deep pools, and troughs or hollows at the water bottom; also in racing water and fast runs below weirs.

Gudgeon *(Gobio gobio).*
Classification: Coarse fish.
Natural home: Slow flowing rivers and canals; also stocked in some pits. Found mainly in England and Ireland.
Notes: Gudgeon are small shoal fish (average weight about 55g) and rarely angled for. In the nineteenth century, cooked

gudgeon was considered a delicacy – it still is in central Europe. Gudgeon feed at the water bottom.

Perch *(Perca fluviatilis).*
Classification: Coarse fish.
Natural home: Lakes, lochs, ponds, rivers, streams and canals; also stocked in some pits and reservoirs.
Popular angling methods: Float fishing; free-lining; legering; paternostering; spinning.

TIPS
Perch feed mainly at mid-water depth, and near the water bottom; though they will rise to take baits and flies at the surface. Fish for perch near reeds, weed beds, submerged tree roots and sunken debris; deep holes and bank undercuts.

Pike *(Esox lucius).*
Classification: Coarse fish.
Natural home: Lakes, lochs, ponds, rivers, streams and canals; also stocked in some pits and reservoirs.
Popular angling methods: Legering; spinning; sink and draw; float fishing; free-lining.
Notes: Pike have large jaws and sharp teeth which may slice through fishing line. Tie an angler's *wire pike trace* between hook and main line. Use an angler's *pike gag* to prop open the pike's mouth securely, while safely removing your hook with a hook disgorger or angler's artery forceps. Wire traces, pike gags, and forceps are sold by tackle dealers.

TIPS
Pike lurk in ambush among weeds, near reeds; behind submerged tree roots, boulders and sunken hefty branches; in underwater holes and gullies; beside inflowing streams, eddies, and at the bottom of deep bays.

Pike like big baits, which they'll seize at any depth, from water top to bottom; big baits fished on, or near, the water bottom, achieve a high success rate.

Roach *(Rutilus rutilus).*
Classification: Coarse fish.
Natural home: Rivers, ponds, lakes, canals; also stocked in pits and reservoirs.
Popular angling methods: Float fishing; free-lining; legering.

TIPS
Roach prefer deep slow-moving or still water, shaded by bankside trees or shrubs. Present your hookbait on, or near, the water bottom – close to reeds, water plants, lily roots, and especially thick weed beds.

Rudd *(Scardinius erythrophthalmus).*
Classification: Coarse fish.
Natural home: Ponds, lakes, canals, rivers; also stocked in pits and reservoirs. Rudd are absent from northern Scotland.
Popular angling methods: Float fishing; free-lining; legering; fly fishing.

TIPS
Rudd are largely mid-water depth and surface feeders. They favour slow moving and still water; can be caught below overhanging trees and shrubs, and near reeds, water plants and lily pads.

Salmon *(Salmo salar).*
Classification: Game fish.
Natural home: The sea, returns to freshwater to spawn (see page 66).
Popular angling methods: Fly fishing; spinning.

TIPS
Salmon, on their way up-river to spawn (see page 66), lie briefly in established and well known resting places (*holding pools*). These "lies" are the best places to catch salmon. Rocky pools of placid water, away from mainstream currents, are favourite salmon lies. To locate the ace "taking places", seek advice and guidance from the water's keeper or

ghillie, or from an experienced local angler. Tackle dealers are pleased to recommend experts you can contact, who will usually expect a fee for their valuable service.

Tench *(Tinca tinca).*
Classification: Coarse fish.
Natural home: Lakes, ponds, rivers, canals; also stocked in pits and reservoirs.
Popular angling methods: Legering; float fishing; free-lining.

TIPS
Tench search for food round the bottom of muddy, reedy and densely weeded bankside shallows. Tench thrive in quiet, slow moving or still water; eat their main meals at dusk and dawn, and offer superb sport in warm summer months, particularly June, July and August.

Trout
Brown trout *(Salmo trutta).*
Sea trout *(Salmo trutta).*
Rainbow trout *(Salmo gairdneri).*
Classification: Game fish.
Natural home: Brown trout live in clean, well-oxygenated water: rivers, streams, lakes and lochs; also stocked in pits and reservoirs.
   Sea trout are brown trout that choose to live and feed at sea. After feeding in the ocean, sea trout grow big and turn silvery in colour; they return to rivers and streams to spawn.
   Rainbow trout, introduced to European waters from North America, are stocked in reservoirs, pits; also some lakes, rivers and streams. Rainbow trout rarely breed in Britain, and live only 5–7 years. However, rainbow trout grow at twice the speed of brown trout, and after 2 years can be in peak sporting condition, and weigh above 2.5kg! Big rainbow trout finally attain weights in excess of 5.5kg.
Popular methods of angling for trout: Fly fishing; spinning; free-lining (upstream worming).

TIPS

Trout feed at all depths. Fish for trout under overhanging trees and shrubs; beneath waterfalls or weirs; in channels between weed beds; deep pools and eddies; near the mouth of inflowing streams or rivulets of water, bankside undercuts, holes or hollows, submerged tree roots; behind boulders; beneath bridges.

Zander *(Stizostedion lucioperca).*
Classification: Coarse fish.
Natural home: Lakes and rivers. Restricted in the U.K. to a few prime locations, notably Woburn Abbey Lakes and the East Anglian fens.
Popular angling methods: Spinning; sink and draw; legering; free-lining.
Notes: Big zanders' sharp teeth can bite through fishing line. To be sure of landing a hooked large zander, tie an angler's *wire trace* between hook and main line. Use a hook disgorger or angler's artery forceps to remove your hook safely from the zander's mouth.

TIPS

Zander packs hunt shoals of small fish. Zander prefer to feed in deep and quiet, open water, where victims can't scoot for cover. Zander scent and track food, so best natural baits are strips or chunks cut from a fresh dead fish (mackerel, herring, sprat), or whole small dead fish; or fat, juicy earthworms. Zander generally dine near the water bottom.

4
TACKLE

Good quality tackle is an important requirement for skilful fishing performance and successful angling results. Begin fishing with basic items of tackle bought from your local specialist tackle shop. Steadily build a complete collection of tip-top tackle to cater for every angling situation you commonly encounter.

Tackle tips and notes on specialist tackle are passed on to you right through this book, to nudge you in the direction of equipment you may find a boon, and passport to trouble-free, first-class sport. However, beware of becoming a reckless and unthinking buyer of tackle you don't know how to use properly, don't need, or will seldom use. Let your good sense make the final ruling regarding tackle purchase.

It pays to chat with *your* friendly tackle dealer, who knows the latest developments in tackle design, and is eager to help you with wise advice on any aspect of angling.

Quality tackle, treated sensibly, lasts a lifetime, and is an excellent investment.

My confession
I must confess, one of the largest sea trout I've seen caught was landed by a 9 year old boy, using a stumpy bamboo garden cane, length of thick green string lashed to a bent safety-pin, and baited with a huge, snake-like earthworm. The lad was surrounded by experienced and well equipped adult anglers, who caught nothing. It was the boy's first ever fishing trip! The moral of this true tale is that tackle and skill won't guarantee big fish. We all need a little bit of luck . . .

Tackle advice
Some items of tackle are suitable for general, all-round freshwater fishing. Specialist tackle for particular methods of angling is mentioned in the Chapter about methods,

beginning on page 24. Explore different types and techniques of fishing before saving money to spend on specialist tackle. Don't specialise until you're certain which angling techniques interest you most.

List of essential tackle.
Rod, about 3m (10 feet) long for general fishing.
Reel – fixed-spool reel, for all-round angling.
Line – sufficient to fill the fixed-spool reel, and of at least 1.36kg (3 lbs) breaking strain (see line strength table on page 20).
Hooks – good quality, *sharp* hooks; a selection of sizes (see Hook Tips on page 35) including: size 16 (small) and size 6 (large).
Weights – packs of assorted size weights for general fishing are available from tackle dealers.

TIP
Aim to use the minimum weight necessary to cast your baited hook the distance required, and hold your bait at the depth and/or position you expect fish to be feeding.
Floats – Watch out! Float buying can become addictive to new *and* experienced anglers. Don't be influenced by pretty colours and unusual shapes. Buy a few floats; learn how to fish them correctly; then add to your float collection only when really necessary.

TIP
Quill floats are ideal general purpose floats; *balsa,* and *stick* floats are best suited to fast or medium-fast flowing rivers or streams. *Antenna*, and *waggler* floats are designed for still or very slow moving waters.

Attach quill, balsa or stick floats to main line at the float's top and bottom.

Attach antenna or waggler floats to main line through the bottom eye only. Lock the float in position by fixing a weight at both sides of the float's bottom eye.

TIP
Use short floats in shallow water; long floats for deep water.

Right strength lines

Breaking strain		Fish
4.53kg (10 lbs)	—	Pike.
2.26kg (5 lbs)	—	Barbel, carp, eel, zander.
1.36kg (3 lbs)	—	Bream, chub, grayling, perch, roach, rudd, tench, trout.
0.90kg (2 lbs)	—	Bleak, dace, gudgeon; small fish of other species.

Please note: These line strengths are recommended where average size fish are expected. Where there's heavy weed and/or big fish are anticipated, increase line strength by about 50%.

Important additional items of tackle

Rod bag, to store and protect your rod.

Reel case, to store and protect your reel.

Hook sharpener – blunt hooks lose fish. Sharpen hooks before use.

Bait boxes – separate boxes for different baits.

Artery forceps or hook disgorger, to remove your hook from the fish's mouth with speed and without harming the fish.

Landing net – adjustable (telescopic) long-handled large landing net, to land hooked big fish that threaten to break your line!

Activity

Floats are easy to make, and home-made floats are great fun to use. After you've made a few floats, you'll soon start designing different models to suit specific waters, and particular ways of presenting your float fished baits to fool suspicious fish.

Tools: a model-maker's *vice* is helpful; a sharp *modelling knife* or suitable penknife; *pliers* for cutting wire float "eyes"; *glasspaper* for smoothing wood to shape and putting a fine finish on rough edges, and a model-maker's *hand drill* or bradawl for boring small diameter holes in wood.

Materials: anything that floats can be fashioned into an effective float, including empty, clear plastic pen tubes. Superb quill floats can be made from the feathers of geese, gulls and crows. Keep large feathers found at the waterside or on countryside rambles – pheasants' tail feather quills float well.

Porcupine and peacock quills are sometimes stocked by specialist tackle dealers for D.I.Y. float makers.

Balsa-wood and sarkandas reed (bought from tackle or model-making shops), and elder pith (cut a few dead stems from elder shrubs or trees in the winter) also produce very buoyant floats.

Model-makers' paints waterproof your floats, and give them a final colourful flourish; fluorescent paints for float tops and tips, bestow that "professional" look, and are available from specialist tackle dealers. Favourite colours include: black, orange, red, and yellow.

Ready-drilled balsa float bodies, dowels, eyes, float caps, and all the latest float making materials are conveniently available from your local tackle dealer.

Three patterns to try
Goose quill float
Extremely useful all-round float.

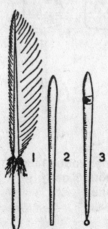

6. Quill float.
1. Wing feather.
2. Stripped quill (about 155mm).
3. Finished float complete with wire eye whipped on with strong thread, and a float cap.

Balsa-wood float

Highly buoyant float (balsa-wood is twice as buoyant as cork); supports a heavy bait in the fast or medium-fast flow of rivers or streams; also effective on still waters.

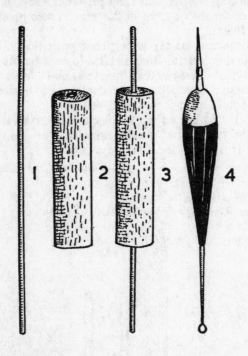

7. Balsa-wood float.
1. Slender rod of cane (about 155mm).
2. Piece of balsa (about 80mm).
3. Balsa glued on cane.
4. The completed float.

Elder pith float
An egg shape float is ideal for fishing the fast runs of rivers and streams.

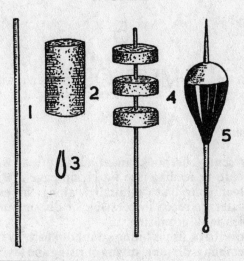

8. Elder pith float
1. Slender rod of cane (about 140mm).
2. Piece of elder pith (about 60mm).
3. Length of fine wire for eye (about 20mm).
4. Elder pith cut into discs, drilled, glued and put on cane.
5. The completed float.

If you relish the fun of crafting D.I.Y. floats, how about making your own fishing rods? Kits, and spares for rod repairs are stocked by, or can be ordered from, specialist tackle dealers.

5
METHODS

Float fishing
Aims
(a) To present your hookbait at any depth at which you expect fish to be feeding (see fig 11, on page 27).
(b) To float your bait "naturally" along the current in flowing water; to reach inaccessible or distant stretches of water which look promising.
(c) To know that a fish is biting your hookbait, by the float's action: trembling, dipping, diving or rising and laying flat on the surface etc.

TIP
If necessary, add sufficient weight to the line beneath your float to *cock* the float: make it stand upright in the water, with the top or tip only showing.
Specialist tackle for float fishing: Float fishing rod, about 3.6m (12 feet) long; fixed-spool reel; floats (see page 19).

Fly fishing
Aim: To present an artificial imitation of a natural fly or insect on or below the water surface.

Dapping: Action of bobbing and skipping a live insect (grasshopper, bluebottle, house-fly, stonefly, beetle etc.) or artificial fly on the water surface by skilfully raising and lowering the rod tip. A float fishing rod of *at least* 3.6m (12 feet) is advisable for dapping at a reasonable distance, as long casts are impractical.

Dry fly fishing: Action of presenting an artificial fly on the water surface.

Wet fly fishing: Action of presenting an artificial fly, insect

9. Dry flies for salmon.
1. Grey Palmer.
2. Cinnamon Sedge.

or water creature (nymph, shrimp, snail etc.) beneath the water surface.

10. Winged wet and dry flies and Spider.
1. Winged wet fly.
2. Winged dry fly.
3. Spider (hackle) dry fly.

Specialist tackle for fly fishing: Fly fishing rod, about 2.6m (8½ feet) long; fly fishing reel; fly-line (to match rod). Also, backing line and leader line: wind about 46m of *backing line* onto your reel. To this tie the fly-line; then tie about 3m of *leader line* to the fly-line. Before fishing, the artificial fly is tied to the end of the leader line.

To work efficiently, your fly rod, reel and line must be correctly balanced. Describe to your local specialist tackle dealer the type of fly fishing you intend doing, and he will expertly guide your choice of *balanced* tackle.

Free-lining

Aim: To present hookbait to fish in the most natural manner possible; without line-restricting float or weights to hinder the bait's progress through the water.

A portion of bread crust, or a maggot chrysalis (*caster*) can be floated on the surface; other baits may be cast and draped across water plants or lily pads, to dangle tantalisingly, slightly below the surface.

Free-lined baits can be cast and allowed to follow the current; or sink slowly in still water to tempt bottom-feeding fish. Tugs or tremors felt along the line signal a bite.

Upstream worming is often an effective way of catching big trout, especially in the clear water of fast-flowing streams; also murky flood waters following heavy rainfall – expect bonus results as the flood water level begins to fall.

Cast the worm *upstream* (up current) and let the current carry it back towards you.

Groundbaiting

Aim: To attract fish to your baited hook.

Method: Mix stale bread crumbs with a few scraps of the hookbait you're using; bind into a *small* ball with water, and gently bowl into the area you intend fishing. Then place your baited hook close to the groundbait.

Note: Groundbait can be used when *float fishing,* or *legering,* or *paternostering,* or *pole fishing.* Groundbait is ineffective in other methods of fishing, and is not used when fishing for trout or salmon.

TIP
Super "secret" groundbait mixtures are sold by specialist tackle dealers. These successful groundbait formulas come neatly packaged with full mixing instructions.

Feeding: After groundbaiting, keep fish dining near your baited hook by *occasional* "feeding" with small or chopped samples of the sort of bait you've spiked on the hook.

TIP
Be stingy with groundbait and loose feed. Fish that stuff themselves with your free offerings won't be hungry for the

bigger bait on your hook!

An angler's catapult enables you to shoot groundbait and/or loose feed a long distance with accuracy.

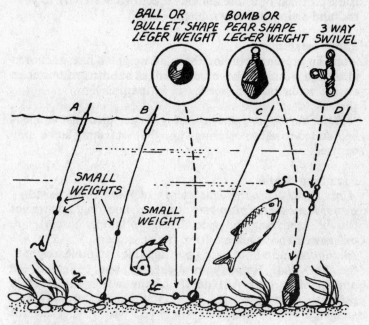

11. Four ways to fish your bait.
A Float fished bait above the water bottom.
B Float fished bait laid at the water bottom.
C Legered bait laid on the water bottom.
D Paternostered bait anchored above weed etc.

Legering

Aim: To present your hookbait, on weighted line, at a precise and fixed position on the water bottom (see fig 11, above). Bites are signalled by tugs or tremors felt along the line. A float may be attached to line when legering in still waters. Specialist bite indicators, for use when legering, are stocked by tackle dealers.

TIP
Use the lightest weight necessary to hold your bait steady at the water bottom.

Specialist tackle for legering: Leger rod, about 3m (10 feet) long; fixed-spool reel; leger weights. Electronic bite alarms that attach to anglers' bank sticks (rod rest supports). Also, rod tip or rod butt bite indicator sections, which fix to your rod and swing to show a bite.

Paternostering
Aim: To present your hookbait, on weighted line, anchored in a fixed position above weed beds or submerged obstacles on the water bottom (see fig 11 on page 27).

Suitable tackle for paternostering: Leger specialist tackle is best suited to paternostering, though float fishing tackle may be used.

Plumbing depths
Aim: To measure the exact depth of water to be fished.
Suitable tackle for plumbing: Any rod, line, float and weight can be used; anglers' special large *plummet weights* are marketed, and available from tackle dealers.
Method: Slide a float onto your line. Tie a suitable weight to the line end. Raise your float up line to equal the approximate (guessed) depth of the water; fix float in position with float cap or elastic band. Carefully cast weighted line to the point where you wish to measure the water depth. Rewind line and adjust float depth-setting until the float tip only is visible slightly above the water surface. Then measure the length of line between your float tip and the weight's base; this distance equals the water's depth.

To measure depths greater than 4m; tie a stop knot (see fig 52, on page 102) to your line, set at the approximated water depth, and leave the float free to slide up the line – guided by the float's bottom eye – until the float is stopped by the stop knot, and your float tip only is visible.

TIP
Cast your weighted line low and accurately across the water, so it enters softly, without a loud "Splosh", which scares fish and angers nearby anglers.

Temperature taking: Plumbing depths is an ideal time to take water temperatures. Attach an *angler's thermometer* to your line near the weight to read the deep water temperature, and raise the thermometer up your line to check and compare near-surface temperature. Anglers' special weighted thermometers are available, which can be used in place of, or in addition to, a plummet weight.

Pole fishing
Aim: To present a float fished bait on a light line, close to, or directly below, the end of your pole.
Method: Line is attached to the pole end. No reel is used.
Specialist tackle for pole fishing: Pole, about 9.5m (31 feet) fully extended; pole lines, floats and weights, wound on special line winders ready for use.

Spinning
Aim: To cast an artificial bait or "lure" that represents a small fish, and rewind the line at varied speeds, coupled with raising and dipping of the rod tip to give your lure the appetising appearance of a wounded and distressed small fish.
   Sink and draw: Method of presenting a natural bait, which is cast; allowed to sink, then drawn towards the surface, and gradually retrieved in a similar fashion to spinning, but with greater emphasis on raising and lowering the rod tip – to sink and draw the bait in a series of jerky movements towards the bankside.

TIP
Spinning is a method that can, when performed with skill, catch large "cannibal" fish of species that enjoy eating young fishes, especially cannibal bream, chub, grayling, perch, pike, roach, trout and zander.
Specialist tackle for spinning: Spinning rod, about 2.13m (7 feet) long; fixed spool reel; lures.

Trolling
Aim: To trail a bait behind a drifting boat. Effective way of catching salmon and trout on large lakes and lochs. Not to be attempted unless you're accompanied by an experienced boat handler; can swim, and wearing a life jacket!

6

BAITS

Fish-catching baits are many and varied. Different species of
fish have particular food preferences, and respond more
readily to some baits than others. Here's a helpful guide to
anglers' consistently successful baits:

Freshwater Bait Guide

Bait		Fish
Bread	—	Barbel/Bream/Carp/Dace/Grayling/Roach/Rudd/Tench.
Cheese	—	Barbel/Carp/Chub/Eel/Roach/Rudd.
Dead Fish	—	Eel/Perch/Pike/Zander.
Fly	—	Barbel/Bream/Carp/Chub/Dace/Grayling/Perch/Salmon/Trout.
Grain	—	Barbel/Chub/Dace/Roach.
Maggot	—	Bream/Carp/Chub/Dace/Perch/Roach/Rudd/Tench/Zander.
Silkweed	—	Barbel/Chub/Dace/Roach/Rudd.
Sweetcorn	—	Carp/Chub/Roach/Rudd/Tench.
Worm	—	Barbel/Bream/Carp/Chub/Dace/Eel/Grayling/Perch/Pike/Roach/Rudd/Salmon/Tench/Trout/Zander.
Lure	—	Bream/Chub/Grayling/Perch/Pike/Roach/Rudd/Salmon/Trout/Zander.

Bread

Use a piece of *crust*, or fluffy bread *flake* from the inside of a
white loaf, or fluffy piece of white bread rolled into a *paste*
with water scooped from the place you're fishing, or a bread
pellet punched from a fresh white loaf with an angler's bread
punch (sold by tackle dealers).

12. Hook baited with bread paste.

Cheese
Use spready or hard cheese, moulded around the hook. Any cheese attracts bites; Cheddar, Gorgonzola and Stilton are great fish favourites (Camembert as a treat on Sundays). The riper and smellier your cheese, the better fish like it!

Dead fish
Fresh sprats, or herrings, or small mackerel, purchased from a fishmonger, or bought frozen from a food store or tackle dealer, are appetizing baits for big predatory fish. The bait fish can be cut into strips, chunks, or fished whole, hooked through the eye sockets.

Fly
A real or artificial fly can be used to catch fish. Juicy, fresh bluebottles, house-flies, craneflies (and lively grasshoppers) are popular with fish. Artificial copies of natural flies and insects are stocked by tackle dealers, or can be made at home (see Chapter 7).

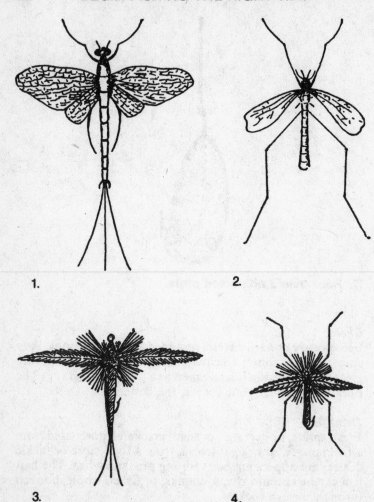

1.

2.

3.

4.

13. Mayfly and Cranefly.
1. Mayfly.
2. Cranefly (Daddy Longlegs).
3. Mayfly (artificial).
4. Cranefly (artificial).

Grain
Hempseed, *patna* rice, pearl barley, tares, wheat etc. To
soften grain ready for fishing, simmer gently in a saucepan of
water for about 20 minutes; then switch off heat. Cover
saucepan; allow to cool before straining softened grain; tip
away surplus water.

Ready cooked grain is stocked by tackle dealers.

Maggot
Maggots (larvae of common blowflies) are sold by specialist
tackle dealers. Maggots become unmoving black chrysalises
before emerging as flies. Anglers call the maggot chrysalis, a
"caster". Casters also catch fish.

14. Hook baited with maggot

Silkweed
Grows on underwater stones and submerged wood.
Carefully gather by hand from shallow water; simply wrap
the soft silkweed around your hook.

Sweetcorn
Buy from your local food store.

Worms
Bloodworms (larvae of midge fly) live in mud at the bottom
of still and slow moving waters. Buy from specialist tackle
dealers.

Brandlings: small red worms, found in compost heaps;
piles of decaying leaves; rotting vegetation etc.

Earthworms (lobworms); long red worms. To find, dig
damp garden soil with a fork (a spade may slice and kill
them); look under large stones; or *in summer:* at night, lay
sacking or a wide black plastic sheet, weighted with a few
heavy stones, over a *watered* close-cut lawn. In the early
morning, collect worms gathered underneath.

Lure
Lures are baits used for *spinning* (see page 29). Some "lures"
are artificial flies used for fly fishing: they resemble no

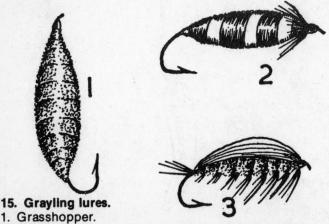

15. Grayling lures.
1. Grasshopper.
2. Finnish lure.
3. Freshwater shrimp.

known natural creature, yet appeal to fish, and invariably bring success.

Hook size

The hook size should match your chosen bait. Tiny baits, like bloodworms, require very small hooks; fat earthworms need large hooks to hold them, and a whole small dead fish must be secured on a big hook.

The sharp hook point should stick right through the bait, so it quickly penetrates the lip of a biting fish as you tighten the line.

TIPS

Select the smallest hook size that suits your bait, then most of the hook is buried in the bait, and disguised from the gaze and touch of inquisitive fish.

Tiny hook size 18 is suitable for bloodworms, brandlings and small bread pellets.

Small hook size 14 or 16 is ideal for bunches of brandlings; maggots, bread, grain, sweetcorn, cheese, silkweed etc.

Large hook size 6 or 8 is best for earthworms; hunks of bread, cheese, silkweed; chunks or strips of fresh fish etc.

Big hook size 1 or 2 is effective when fishing with whole small dead fish.

TIP

Be generous when baiting your hook. Big fish prefer bumper baits!

Buy anglers' bait boxes to keep live bait fresh and wriggly. Put different live baits in separate containers; store in a cool place away from heat, and shaded from sunshine – especially while fishing. Live baits may droop and die if they get too hot!

Activity

Make a record in your angling notebook of baits that catch fish. When the season ends, draw a chart showing the degree of success each bait achieved with different species of fish. You may be surprised at the results!

See my last season's freshwater bait chart on page 36.

✳ = GOOD ✓ = EFFECTIVE ✗ = POOR	BREAD	CHEESE	FISH- DEAD SPRAT HERRING ETC.	MAGGOT	SWEETCORN	WORM	SPINNER SPOON PLUG ETC.
BARBEL	✳	✳		✓	✗	✳	
BREAM	✳	✓		✳	✓	✳	✓
CHUB	✳	✳		✓	✳	✳	✓
EEL		✳	✳	✗		✳	
PIKE			✳			✳	✳
ROACH	✳	✳		✳	✳	✳	✓
TENCH	✳	✓		✳	✳	✳	

16. Notebook: Freshwater bait chart.

7

FLY-TYING

Fly-tying is a simple and rewarding skill, well worth learning. To hook a fish with your own home-made fly is an electrifying thrill you'll always remember. Once the basics of fly-tying are understood and practised, you'll quickly develop your own technique and style, and maybe design your own artificial flies!

The outward appearance of natural flies, insects and tiny water creatures can be closely imitated or approximated, or disregarded in favour of the imaginative creation of a non-existent creature – with built-in big fish meal appeal! Successful original fly patterns are sometimes named after their inventors.

All tools and materials for fly-tying are stocked by, or can be ordered from, specialist tackle dealers.

Tools
Desirable tools include: a fly-tyer's *vice* to grip hooks, leaving your hands free! Special fly-tyer's *scissors;* hackle-holding *hackle pliers,* and a *dubbing needle* for teasing a "hairy" look in finished fly bodies; guiding and positioning threads etc.

Materials
Feathers, furs and/or man-made fibres, wools, tying silks, threads, wires and tinsels of selected types and sizes.

Also necessary is fly-tying *wax*, to wax silk thread before tying; fly-tying *varnish* to seal, gloss and protect the *head* of flies, and dry-fly oil to coat and waterproof the body, wings and tail of completed *dry flies* before drying and storing ready for use.

Fly-tying kits
Your local specialist tackle dealer will stock, or should be delighted to order, an inexpensive beginner's fly-tying kit,

containing tools, materials and full instructions.

TIP
Buy best quality *sharp* hooks. Sizes 14 or 16 for trout flies; sizes 10 or 12 for sea trout flies; sizes 6 or 8 for salmon flies.

Fly-words		Meaning
Hackle	—	Bushy collar of feathers below the hook's eye.
Hair-wing	—	Strands of spiky hair tied as wings, instead of soft feather wings.
Spider	—	An artificial fly resembling no known insect; attracts fish all season because it looks "alive", insect-like and visually appealing (to fishes).

Preparing feathers

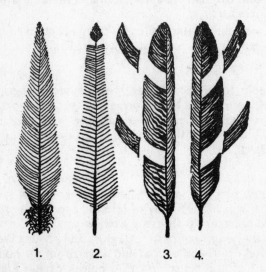

1.   2.   3. 4.

17. Preparing Feathers.

No. 1 of fig 17 shows an unprepared *hackle* feather; in No. 2 the feather is prepared by stroking the fibres downwards towards the butt, making them stand out at right angles. Select and carefully remove the brightest and best formed fibres to make a "hackle".

Nos. 3 and 4 show two separate feathers chosen to make a fly's *wings*, with the best sections cut away to form the "wings" of a winged fly.

Two knots

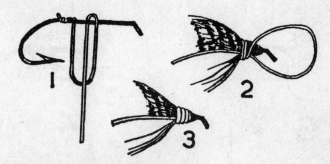

18. Half-hitch and whip-finish knots.
1. Half-hitch knot.
2. Start of whip-finish knot at head of fly.
3. The completed whip-finish knot.

Begin fly-tying, and end each stage of tying, with a neat half-hitch. Finish the completed fly with a *tidy* whip-finish knot at the head, and seal with fly-varnish.

March Brown Spider (wet or dry)
A most effective trout fly; hooks fish throughout the season.

Tail: Three fibres of a partridge feather.
Body: Brown wool with fine oval gold tinsel.
Hackle: Brown partridge hackle feather (soft-fibred hen hackle for "wet" spider; stiff-ribbed fibre cock hackle for "dry" spider).
Tying silk: Yellow.
Hooks: 14 or 16.

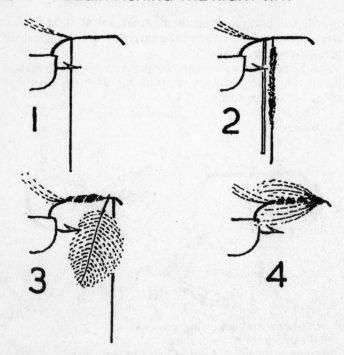

19. March Brown Spider (wet).

1. Three fibres of a partridge feather are tied in for the tail.
2. A length of fine oval gold tinsel is waiting to be wound round body and brown wool has been spun on to the tying silk.
3. Body is complete and a partridge hackle feather is ready to be wound at head.
4. The finished fly.

Mallard And Claret, winged wet fly
Highly successful fly for catching sea trout, or any big trout living in reservoirs, lakes or lochs.

Tail: Three fibres from the tippet feather of a golden pheasant.
Body: Claret wool ribbed with fine oval gold tinsel.
Hackle: Claret coloured hen hackle.

Wings: Brown mallard.
Tying silk: Claret.
Hooks: 10 or 12 for sea trout; size 14 for trout.

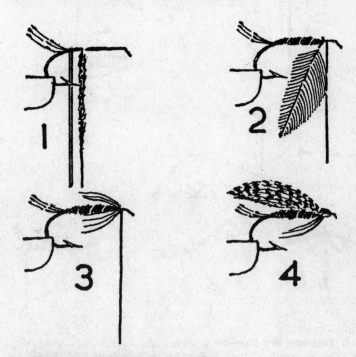

20. Mallard and Claret sea trout fly.

1. Tail of golden pheasant tippet is tied in, a length of fine oval gold tinsel is waiting to be wound and some claret wool has been spun on to the tying silk.
2. Body is complete and a claret hen hackle is waiting to be wound.
3. Hackle is in position.
4. The finished fly with brown mallard wings.

Hair-winged trout flies
Can be tied with a single and sparse, long hair-wing, and fished wet (beneath the surface); or tied with 2 sparse, outstretched hair-wings, and fished dry (on the surface).

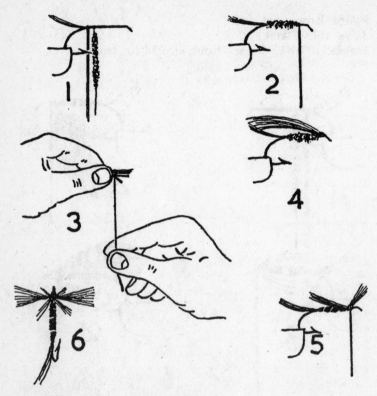

21. Wet and dry hair-wing flies.
1. Tail of squirrel hair is tied in, a length of gold tinsel is hanging and some grey wool is on tying silk.
2. The body is complete.
3. A sparse bunch of squirrel hair is tied in.
4. The finished fly.
5. Putting hair-wings on a dry fly.
6. A finished hair-wing dry fly.

Tail: Three or four hairs from a grey squirrel tail.
Body: Grey wool, ribbed with fine gold oval tinsel; the wool to be teased out between the ribbing.
Wings: Grey squirrel.
Tying silk: Grey.
Hooks: Size 14 or 16 for trout; size 10 or 12 for sea trout.

Activity
Keep a record in your angling notebook of flies that catch you fish. After the season's end, make a chart showing the level of success each fly achieved.

See my last season's trout fly chart below.

✳ = GOOD ✓ = EFFECTIVE ✗ = POOR	BLACK SPIDER (WET)	COACHMAN (DRY)	COCH-Y-BONDHU (DRY)	GREENWELLS GLORY (WET OR DRY)	RED PALMER (WET OR DRY)	TUP'S INDISPENSABLE (DRY)	WICKHAM'S FANCY (DRY)
MARCH		✓	✗		✳		
APRIL		✓	✓	✓	✳	✳	✗
MAY	✗	✓	✓	✳	✳	✳	✓
JUNE	✓	✳	✓	✳	✳	✳	✳
JULY	✳	✳	✓	✓	✳	✳	✳
AUGUST	✓	✳			✳	✳	✳
SEPTEMBER	✗	✓	✓			✳	✗

22. Notebook: Trout fly chart.

8

STREAMS, BROOKS AND BURNS

Streams are small rivers; the fast moving clear waters supply fish with plenty of oxygen and food. Brooks are little streams. Slender burns snake and plunge down mountain slopes. A "burn" or "beck" is a small stream.

Streams that begin high up in mountains are inhabited almost solely by the hardy and energetic brown trout, who love rapid well-oxygenated water. Other freshwater fish join trout at lower levels, where currents are less violent.

Streams are perfect places to learn fishing, and the wary, fighting-fit fish give excellent sport. Many streams hold surprisingly large fish, but you've got to be wily and skilful to catch them. I've caught eels weighing 1.5kg in a forest stream you could step over. And then there was the really BIG one that escaped . . . !

FASCINATING FACTS
The fierce night-feeding freshwater crayfish *(Potamobius pallipes),* who is closely related to the lobster, often loses limbs in underwater fights with marauding fish and other crayfish. The remarkable crayfish is able to replace lost legs or claws with new-grown limbs!

Fossilised impressions of the Mayfly show it has existed for at least 325 million years. Today there are over 1,500 different species of Mayfly worldwide.

Stream, brook and burn fish
Streams and brooks: Chub, dace, eel, grayling, perch, pike, brown trout. Some streams that flow into the sea are entered by sea trout and salmon at spawning time.
Burns: Mainly brown trout.

23. A typical Snowdon Valley stream.

24. Brown Trout.

Right stream, brook and burn methods include: Float fishing; fly fishing; free-lining; legering; spinning.

Great spots to fish
*Deep pools of slow moving water.
*Deep scoured bankside undercuts, where shallow fast water has eaten down into the bank and underwater bed, slowing into a deep, lazy, sleeve-shaped run.
*Beneath overhanging shrubs and/or tree branches, and near submerged tree roots.

25. Deep pool in the higher reaches of a mountain stream.

*Near water plants and between clumps of weed.
*Where inflowing trickles and rivulets of water drain or flow into the main body of water.
*Swirling and circling eddies which draw and trap food from the main current.
*The oxygen-rich pools of water below cascading waterfalls.
*Alongside and behind boulders that break the current and give fish a sheltered spot from which to seize passing food.
*The stretch of water immediately before the stream flows into a river or lake; the meeting point of the waters, and slightly beyond, into the river or lake.

TR = TROUT →ᐟ = CURRENT ◎ = DEEP POOLS

26. Map of trout stream.

Stream, brook and burn success hints
1. Sneak towards the spot you intend fishing from *downstream* (down current). Fishes face upstream, into the current, to catch food carried towards them, and are less likely to notice you approaching from behind – providing you're quiet!
2. Cast your baited hook ahead of the place where you expect fish to be feeding, and let the bait drift naturally to them. Be patient; allow your hookbait to flow past you; guide it towards the bankside. Pause; watch for signs of the

bait being investigated by a pursuing fish (bobbing float; twitch or tug on line; swirl of water betraying the fish's presence etc). When satisfied no fish has followed your bait, reel-in; check bait is intact and looks fish-attracting good – if not, rebait hook with fresh bait. Then cast again!

3. On bright, sunny days, fish feed in deep water, and hide among water plants, hunting in shallow areas after dark and at first light.

4. Legering (see page 27) bait in a deep pool or run of water may catch a big fish lying low and feeding deep until after dark.

5. On dull days fish are often active from dawn to mid-morning and from early evening into the night.

6. Fish feast during and after rainfall, which washes insects and grubs into the water.

7. Flood waters force fish to shelter in bankside bays and hollows from strong central currents. Fish take advantage of this opportunity to search for food washed into the water from newly eroded bankside soil.

8. When fish are rising to snatch hatching flies from the water surface, attach a real insect or artificial fly to your line and thrill to the excitement of dapping or dry fly fishing (see page 24).

TACKLE + TIPS

In addition to the main items of tackle recommended in Chapter 4 you may find some of these extras worth buying or saving-up for.

● A stout pair of leather walking boots support your ankles and protect the soles of your feet (wear 2 pairs of socks) from bruising when striding and scrambling long distances between fish-holding pools and deep runs.

● Polarised sun-glasses reduce glare from water and enable you to see "hidden" fish skulking at the water bottom

● An angler's haversack holds spare tackle and snacks; slips over your shoulder and is a comfy way to carry angling oddments.

● Special many-pocketed fishing jackets and waistcoats supply handy places to lodge nick-nacks ready for easy access when required.

27. The Inver – one of Scotland's many picturesque streams.

● Remember to take insect repellent with you in the summer, or you'll be bitten while waiting for bites!

Stream, brook and burn nature trail
Mountain burns and streams race and tumble over rocks covered with moss, liverwort and algae growth. Stonefly and mayfly nymphs wedge against stones. In slower streams and brooks, water plants have a chance to spread and flourish:

watercress, crowfoot and yellow-flowering kingcups. Watch for sticklebacks, minnows and the small bullhead (*Cottus gobio*) or "Miller's Thumb". Brilliant-coloured kingfishers; dippers and grey wagtails are seen beside streams. Near woodlands or moors, watch for the majestic kestrel or "windhover", hovering into the wind – eyes sharp for prey (shrews, frogs, voles, mice etc).

28. Kestrel.

9
PONDS AND PITS

Most ponds and all pits are man-made and conveniently close to places people live. Easily accessible ponds and pits are typically well stocked with strong fish that give great sport. Ponds once were valuable to villages as a source of water for the population; passing travellers, their horses, and herds bound for market. *Stewponds* were stocked with fish to catch for food – bream, carp, tench and eels being welcome favourites; pike was considered a delicacy! *Millponds* provided millers with power to grind flour for daily bread. *Farm ponds* supplied water for farm animals, and *ornamental ponds* were excavated on private land to look nice for the wealthy landowners and their guests. Many ponds are currently open to the public for fishing.

Old clay pits *(marl pits)* quarried for "marl", a chalky clay, and more recent *gravel pits* provided materials for the building industry. The disused pits now make suitable homes for introduced species of fish.

Ponds and pits are happy habitats and prolific breeding grounds for a rich assortment of water life.

FASCINATING FACT
Today's popular Norfolk Broads waterways have resulted from flooded channels, originally hand-cut by villagers in the Middle Ages, to remove *peat* valued as slow-burning fuel for cooking and heat.

Pond and pit fish: Carp, roach, tench, rudd, bream, eel, perch, pike, chub (sometimes); brown trout and rainbow trout in some waters.
Right pond and pit methods include: Float fishing; free-lining; paternostering; legering.
Great spots to fish
*Seek undiscovered "hotspots" hidden below dense flesh-scratching bankside shrubs. Weave your way thoughtfully

29. Pond life.

1. Bulrush.
2. Iris.
3. Swift.
4. Swallow
5. Midges.
6. Dragonfly.
7. Water crowfoot.
8. Pond skater.
9. Waterlily.
10. Water scorpion.
11. Water beetle.
12. Perch.
13. Water spider and 'air bell' home.
14. Frog.
15. Ramshorn snail.
16. Canadian pondweed.
17. Hornwort.
18. Newt.
19. Eel.
20. Stickleback's nest.
21. Stickleback.

through or around; don't hack a trail into screening vegetation. Leave all undisturbed and keep your secret hotspot safe!

*Beneath overhanging tree/shrub branches, especially those swarming with insects, or heavy with ripe berries.

*Just beyond bank edge reeds and rushes; weed beds and water plants.

*Far from the bank on noisy, angler-packed ponds and pits, and waters with few water's edge aquatic plants.
*Where the breeze-driven surface of deep water licks against a bank edge, lapping soil and insects into the water.
*Deep underwater holes and hollows.

Activity
Draw in your notebook, a map of the pond or pit you fish. Mark the position of important bankside features; aquatic plants etc. Include approximate and/or precise plumbed depths (see page 28) and the places fish have been caught (see fig 30, below). Your map will soon prove a supreme source of information; a reliable at-a-glance guide to help predict where to fish successfully for different species.

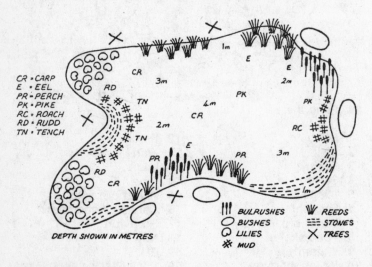

30. Map of pond.

Pond and pit success hints
1. Pond and pit fish watch for warning movements or shadows above them. Tread lightly and stay well back from the water's edge. Slight bankside sounds scare away fish in the quiet of still waters. Stay hidden behind shielding reeds, shrubs or trees where possible.
2. Be prepared to wait patiently for long periods; don't

repeatedly re-bait and recast your line. Pond and pit fish search steadily for food and given time, will find your hookbait. Because there's no current to carry the bait away, cautious fish observe and inspect the bait before mouthing it.
3. Free-lined (see page 26) baits, fished without weights or float, can be spectacularly successful. Pond and pit fish are quick to see weights and feel the unnatural pull of float or weights on line and may avoid or immediately drop the bait. Where free-lining is not possible or desirable, use the smallest float and/or weights necessary to carry the bait where you want to put it.
4. A hooked fish rockets straight towards underwater cover: weed bed, water-lily, tree roots etc. Always work out where hooked fish are likely to run *before* fishing, and steer them from the safety of line-breaking underwater snags.
5. A *scattering* of groundbait attracts tiny fish to the area of your choice. The sound of these small fish feeding excites big fish to investigate. Large fish will make a bee-line for your big hookbait.
6. Use generous portions of hookbait. Big pond and pit fish seldom bother with insubstantial offerings, and permit small fish to mop them up. Small fishes can't swallow large baits and leave them for big fish.
7. *In summer*, on sunny days, dawn, dusk and after dark are the best times to expect good catches. On dull summer's days, begin fishing mid-morning or late afternoon/evening. Hot weather entices fish to the surface, away from pond and pit bottoms. Fish can be seen sunning their backs and rolling round in the shady shelter of water plants, but they don't get hungry until the temperature drops – then feed ravenously!
8. *In winter*, pond and pit fish stay down and reduce feeding. Best catches are probable when the water is warmest, between 10 a.m. and 4 p.m. Midday until 2 p.m. is a favourite time for fish to pursue their winter lunch.

TACKLE + TIPS
In addition to the main items of tackle recommended in Chapter 4, you may find some of these extras worth buying or saving-up for.
●Anglers' featherweight folding seats; tough tackle box/ seats, and fishing stool rucksacks offer comfortable support

to aching limbs on long bankside vigils.

● A telescopic (extendable) long-handled large landing net is a must on waters holding heavy fish – otherwise *your* record breaking catch may escape... and who will believe your story of the monster that got away?

● An angler's special thermometer, attached to your line when plumbing depths (see page 28) enables you to note water temperatures at different places and water levels. This information, jotted in your notebook, and coupled with details of catches, weaves a pattern of facts that in time tell you what water conditions favour good catches of which species of fish in a specific location. You'll probably find few fish feed if the water surface temperature tops 20°C or falls below 5°C.

● Rod rests allow short snack breaks in long fishing sessions. An *electronic bite alarm* fitted to the rod rest alerts us to the inevitable fish's bite that always occurs when we've a sandwich in one hand and mug of coffee in the other.

● Anglers wanting to float fish bait after dark can choose from a variety of special floats that glow brightly above water, all night if required.

Pond and pit nature trail
Alder, birch, grey poplar and willow trees often ring the water, which is fringed by grasses, sedges and rushes. Look for common reed, bur-reed and reedmace (bulrushes); iris (yellow flag), sweet flag and arrowhead; surface-carpeting duckweed, broken by floating white-flowering frogbit and yellow or white water-lilies.

The thriving plant and insect life in well-oxygenated ponds and pits nourishes fish, frogs and newts. Watch for coots, herons, great crested grebes, mallards, moorhens, swallows, swifts and teal.

10

HOW TO SET UP
AN AQUARIUM

Learn to know and care for pond creatures and water plants; keep some briefly as honoured guests in the luxurious setting of a well-looked-after home aquarium; then return your new found aquatic friends to their original watery home.

Angler's aquarium aims
*To observe closely water life behaving "naturally" at our leisure.
*To note the normal behaviour and any apparent peculiarities.
*To sketch in detail plants and creatures, and check names and species are identified correctly. A magnifying glass assists close scrutiny; a microscope is ideal for examination of microscopic organisms: algae, amoeba etc.
*To watch for changes in the behaviour of water life which can be linked to variation in light, temperature, time etc.
*To identify individual behaviour of different species of fish and insect. Do they establish and defend a special territory (where, how, why) or do they roam freely? At what depth do they prefer living/feeding – surface, mid-water, bottom – or is there no preference? At what times do they seem most active/hungry – is there a regular pattern? What are the favourite foods – listed in order of response? How do they take food – seize, approach cautiously, play with before eating? Is food (name type) swallowed whole/torn? Etc., etc.
*To describe any growth, development or changes in water life during period spent in aquarium.

TIP
Borrow books from your local public library to help identify water life and assist your research and study. Spend a pleasant hour or two in the library's reference section. The

librarian should be happy to guide your choice of suitable books.

Collecting
Collect only *stillwater* life from the safe shallow parts of ponds. Creatures netted from the flowing water of streams may die in unmoving aquarium water. Go with a friend – wear old clothes. Be careful near the waterside... don't wade, or lean over deep water! Take care not to trample flowers or uproot water plants. Gently return unwanted water life.

Equipment
Long handled fine-mesh net.
Large plastic bucket.
Also useful: one or two plastic containers with snap-on lids (pin-pricked with air holes); plastic sieve or tea strainer (bought for this purpose) and a plastic spoon.

To set up aquarium
Place the aquarium somewhere cool, away from direct sunlight. Level 25mm of rinsed aquarium gravel along the bottom. Add a few washed large stones to give protection and cover, and cleaned pieces of branch or wood to project above the water for clinging and climbing insects and amphibians (newts, tiny frogs). Three-quarters fill with tap water. Allow to settle for 24 hours before digging the roots or stems of a few oxygenating plants into the gravel.

TIP
Buy fish tank gravel and oxygenating plants from a pet shop or aquatic specialist shop.

Leave aquarium for 7–14 days for plants to begin rooting; then look for suitable aquatic guests for your new water life hotel.

TIP
A close fitting aquarium lid (bought from a pet shop or specialist dealer) keeps out dust and cats!

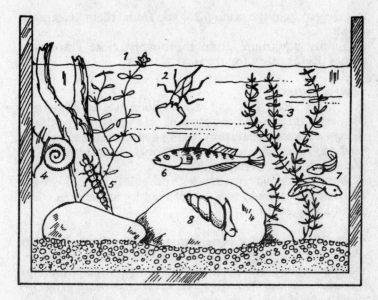

31. Aquarium.

1. Water starwort.
2. Water scorpion.
3. Canadian pondweed.
4. Ramshorn snail.

5. Caddis larva.
6. Stickleback.
7. Tadpoles.
8. Great pond snail.

Rules
1. Don't overcrowd the aquarium.
2. Do keep a varied selection of aquatic creatures; be prepared for *carnivores* to kill and eat fellow guests. The life and death struggle you witness is a normal part of everyday living in their natural environment. Reduce death in your aquarium by limiting the number of carnivores kept, and by feeding regularly, but *sparingly* with pet fish food (including live Daphnia) recommended for fish fry and small fish.
3. Clean green algae from the aquarium sides with an inexpensive special scraping tool (stocked by pet and aquarist shops).
4. When satisfied with your observations and records (probably after 3 or 4 weeks) remove water creatures and

release gently in the same place you found them. Retain the plants.
5. Empty aquarium; clean thoroughly; rinse gravel and plants. Refill ready for the next arrivals.

Golden Rules
A. Most small fish and insects soon feel at home in a properly maintained aquarium. However, any clearly distressed water creature suffering due to confinement (not feeding, becoming feeble etc.) should be returned to its watery home soon as possible.
B. Never mix pond creatures with pet goldfish. Goldfish may eat them, and could also be infected by bacteria to which pond life is immune.

Water life suitable for aquarium (see NOTE at bottom of list).
Plants include: Canadian pondweed; elodea; hornwort; starwort; vallisneria; duckweed (floating); frogbit (floating).
Creatures include: Caddis-fly larvae (herbivores); damselfly nymph (carnivore); dragonfly nymph (carnivore); freshwater shrimps (scavengers); great diving beetle (carnivore); great pond snail (herbivore); newt (carnivore – needs some large stones and pieces of wood projecting above water); ramshorn snails (herbivores); sticklebacks (carnivores); tadpoles (herbivores; develop into carnivores); water boatman (carnivore – they bite!); water mite (carnivore); water scorpion (carnivore); water beetles (herbivores); water spiders (carnivores); whirligig beetle (carnivore).

NOTE: *Carnivores* eat other creatures.
          Herbivores eat plants.
          Scavengers eat dead and decaying matter.

11

CANALS

Artificial waterways designed for travel or irrigation are called "canals".

Before the faster and more economical railways were constructed, several thousand miles of canals were cut across Britain to provide easy passage for barges laden with heavy cargoes of coal, ore, grain etc.

Most U.K. canals were dug during the eighteenth and early nineteenth centuries to serve the busy industrial centres of the Midlands and North of England.

Canals exist today in many parts of Britain, and can offer good fishing.

32. The canal near Tring.

FASCINATING FACTS

A canal 80km long and 20m wide was built between Bavian and Nineveh (Assyria) in 700 B.C., in the reign of the Assyrian King, Sennacherib. The canal included a dam and sophisticated sluice gates to control the water level.

The Romans built canals in Britain to move troops and supplies. The Roman Fosse Dyke connecting the Rivers Trent and Witham is still in use!

Canal fish: Roach, gudgeon, bream, tench, perch, rudd, eel, pike, carp.

Right canal methods include: Float fishing; free-lining; legering.

Great spots to fish

*Near weeds, rushes and water plants, where insects and tiny fish fry gather.

*Inlet pipes, and inflowing streams of water, which tumble oxygen and food into the canal.

*Outflow pipes that create stirring and whirling currents that trap food.

*Holes and hollows in the bank where eels, perch and pike may lurk.

*Deep channels where boats skirt canal bends.

*Deep water and pools near lock gates.

*Barge mooring areas – wide, deep hunting grounds for feeding fish.

Canal success hints

1. Use a light line in clear water: 907g (2 lbs) breaking strain for general fishing. Heavier line is detected and avoided by shy canal fish. Stronger line may be necessary where big fish are expected.

2. When float fishing, attach few (if any) weights to the line – bunched mainly beneath the float. Canal fish notice the unnatural plunge and awkward movement of bait hindered by weighted line.

3. Use very small amounts of groundbait; occasionally scatter a few samples of your hookbait *(loose feed)* to attract fish and keep them feeding close to your baited hook. There is little or no current in canals to disperse and carry away surplus groundbait and loose feed; fish soon eat their fill and

left-overs decompose on the canal bottom.
4. Best canal baits: Worms or maggots in cloudy water; bread in clear water and freezing winter water.
5. *In summer*, pleasure boats on canals disturb fish and churn water cloudy. To beat bothersome boats and catch frightened fish:
(a) Fish early in the morning and/or late evening, when boat traffic is minimal.
(b) Present your hookbait along the shelves on the side of the canal. Fishes move away from the deep channel coursed by boats and rise in the cloudy water to feed round shelves formed by boat swell, on tiny creatures washed into the canal or swirled from their hiding places. Some large fish feed contentedly less than 650mm beneath the water surface.

On canals free of boat traffic, fishes gather in deep water to seek food in daytime; though they often snoop beside quiet banks at dawn and sunset. *In winter*, fishes dive deep for warmth; eat little, and to conserve energy, don't travel fast or far. An increase in water temperature encourages renewed interest in feeding.
6. Keep hooked fish below the surface; reel-in quickly and lift or net your fish from the water with a deliberate and steady action. Hooked fish splashing on the surface, and angler's jerky landing movements frighten away nervous fish shoals.

TACKLE + TIPS
In addition to the main items of tackle recommended in Chapter 4, you may find some of these extras worth buying or saving-up for.

● Buy an angler's special catapult to shoot small samples of bait accurately across the canal when fishing the far side, and attract hungry fish to your hookbait.
● An angler's bread punch instantly produces perfect bread pellets that stay on your hook after casts, and don't fast dissolve in the water!
● In windy weather, the pole (see page 29) enables you to present bait direct to fish in a natural way, without line dragging on the choppy canal surface, or transmitting wind-plucked warnings along line to fish investigating bait.

● Polarised sun-glasses make it possible for you to peer deep into clear canal water and see feeding shoals, and big fishes' secret hiding places.

Canal nature trail
Plush towpath growth of grasses and sedges; water's edge sweet flag, reedmace (bulrushes) and water-lilies. Watch for frogs, water voles and varied bird-life, including the reed and sedge warblers. Canal water is a perfect home for stillwater insects.

12

RIVERS

A river is a large stream of water. Rivers can be slow-moving, broad and deep; or fast flowing and shallow. Many rivers begin as narrow hill streams, rolling downland, where they slow, broaden and deepen as they spread towards the sea.

The same river may change character several times along its length, requiring the angler to be adaptable and adopt different methods and skills to be sure of success.

Some rivers end their run in lakes or marshes; merge with other rivers, or pass through their own estuary mouth into the ocean.

The best known river in England is the River Thames, which rises in the Cotswolds, twists its way eastwards and

33. The Thames, near Windsor.

after a long winding journey, flows through London and into the North Sea.

The longest river in Britain is the River Severn, which rises high up on the Plynlimon ridge in central Wales and flows 290km into the Bristol Channel and Atlantic Ocean.

FASCINATING FACT
The magnificent Atlantic Salmon *(Salmo salar)* spends its adult life in the ocean, returning to freshwater rivers and streams to spawn; then attempts the arduous journey back downstream to the sea. It is illegal to kill thin and exhausted spawned salmon, known as "kelts". Some salmon die before reaching their salt water home after spawning. Males are less likely to survive than females.

34. Salmon.

Salmon, driven by instinct, are tenacious in their fight to reach shallow gravel spawning beds – often far up isolated hill streams. A high proportion of salmon return to the exact location where they themselves hatched. Salmon have been known to travel 100km a day for 12 days to reach their spawning grounds. Powerful, leaping salmon can be seen climbing, step-by-step, rapids and waterfalls.

35. Salmon running up a Scottish Highland river.

Salmon don't normally feed between leaving and returning to the sea; anglers' flies or baits are possibly seized in irritation, because salmon find their presence annoying.

After hatching, young salmon spend 2 to 4 years in freshwater, then swim out to sea. It's a further 2 to 5 years before they return to spawn. The precise travel and feeding patterns of ocean salmon shoals is not fully understood. Some salmon shoals feed near Greenland, and tagged adults have been tracked moving from Norway to spawn in Scotland.

River fish: Barbel, bleak, bream, carp, chub, dace, eel, grayling, gudgeon, perch, pike, roach, rudd, tench, brown trout. The rainbow trout and zander live in a few rivers; some rivers are visited by salmon and sea trout at spawning time.

Right river methods include: Float fishing; free-lining; legering; paternostering; spinning; fly fishing.

Great spots to fish
*Beneath overhanging trees or shrubs.
*Near water plants and weed beds.
*Streamy runs of fast water between weed beds.
*Just above food-rich, but densely-weeded patches of river bed, using the *paternoster* (see page 28) method of fishing.
*Slightly beyond submerged tree roots in deep runs of water.
*Near sunken tree trunks, or other fish-harbouring debris.
*Curling and circling water of an eddy.
*Shallow bankside runs, sheltered from strong currents, where insects breed and fish fry cavort.
*Deep holes or hollows in the river bed.
*Deep stretches of smooth-flowing water.
*Close to the bank in steady, deep water, away from fast flowing mainstream river currents.
*The inside of river bank bends, where food is deposited by the current.
*Pools below weirs and waterfalls.
*The area where river-mouth water flows into a lake; or the confusion of currents where two rivers meet.
*Beneath bridges, where fish feel secure; especially old stone

36. River Brathay, Lake District.

bridges, whose small cracks and crevices are home to teeming insects that regularly "plop" into the water.

37. Chagford Bridge, Dartmoor.

River success hints

1. Look for quiet stretches of water away from riverside noise and bustle.

2. When using groundbait (see page 26) and loose feed to attract fish, throw upstream (up current) so it drifts down current towards you, and settles at the spot you're fishing.

3. Always keep your line taut to prevent hooked fish diving into weed beds or under tree roots to tangle and snap the line.

4. *In winter*, fish stay out of strong, rain-swollen currents; hide low in bankside holes, hollows and gullies; quiet bays; deep and placid spreads of water, and peaceful eddies protected from chill winds by steep banks.

5. Fish are reluctant to expend energy chasing food in winter, so place your hookbait close to the spot you calculate fish to be lying, and expect to wait longer than usual for bites. For best results, present your hookbait on, or near, the water bottom.

6. On mild winter's days fishes may start feeding early or mid-morning. In cold weather, early or mid-afternoon is a sensible time to begin fishing on many rivers. Late afternoon/early evening can be rewarding. In *freezing* weather, fish might not feed for days! A bright, sunny spell and thaw revives sport.

7. The thunderous drumming of heavy rain or hail puts fish down deep, and temporarily off their food. However, as the rain eases, fish cruise close to the bank, seeking food (worms, insects, grubs etc.) washed into the water.

8. Rivers fish best at "normal" water level. Floods and drought-level low water upset fishes; inhibit them from feeding, and adversely affect sport.

9. *In summer,* fish are widely distributed round the river; hunt food at varying depths; chase and track food; explore and sometimes adopt new feeding grounds. Fish begin feeding at dawn and finish early or mid-morning. They feed again from late afternoon or early evening until dusk and after dark; often late into the night.

10. Summertime low-level clear water, gives us an ideal opportunity to eye the river bed, and map in our notebook interesting features (submerged obstacles, weed beds, boulders, tree roots, holes, gullies etc.) ordinarily masked from view by deep water.

Activity

Draw in your notebook, a map of the river you fish. Mark information *you* consider important and useful. Aim to include facts that will help improve your catches: water depths; position of weed beds, hollows and holes; direction of main current and eddies. Places particular species of fish have been caught; spied lurking, or seen to feed. Refer to my river map, fig 38.

TACKLE + TIPS

In addition to the main items of tackle recommended in Chapter 4, you may find some of these extras worth buying or saving-up for.

● An angler's eye-shade reduces glare on bright days; protects eyes from strain, and aids our focus and concentration on the water.

● Anglers' special catapults make easy otherwise difficult long distance groundbaiting (see page 26) and feeding.

● A pair of rod rests allow you *occasionally* to relax your arms, and take a break.

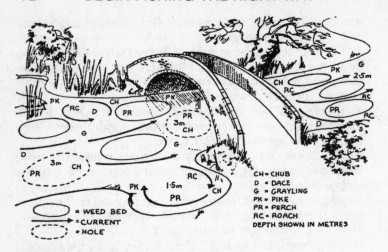

CH = CHUB
D = DACE
G = GRAYLING
PK = PIKE
PR = PERCH
RC = ROACH
DEPTH SHOWN IN METRES

= WEED BED
= CURRENT
= HOLE

38. Map of river.

● A long-handled (telescopic) large landing net, is essential for successfully landing hooked large fish.

● A *spare reel spool*, ready-loaded with extra-strong line, is easily fastened to your fixed-spool reel in place of the spool and line you generally use, should you unexpectedly discover the lair of a BIG fish!

● A tackle box, neatly packed, is a boon to the angler in a hurry – who can quickly find tackle wanted. The rigid box prevents floats getting snapped and tackle damaged.

● A spacious rod holdall is an efficient way for the serious angler to store, carry and safeguard several different specialist rods; together with rod rests, landing net and folded angler's umbrella.

● Anglers who enjoy regularly taking part in fishing matches, find a carry-all bag, and bait apron invaluable.

● A reliable spring-balance, and angler's weigh net, give an accurate bankside reading of a big fish's weight, before its safe return to the water.

River nature trail
Alder, goat willow and white willow trees grow beside rivers. The bankside may be bordered by great willow-herb (purple-pink flowers); meadowsweet (cream-white flowers) and purple loosestrife (red-purple flowers). Water's edge plants

might include the bur-reed (green flowers); iris (yellow flag – yellow flowers) and arrowhead (white flowers with purple centres).

Rivers are busy thoroughfares for many animals, birds and insects. Check soft earth for prints of fox, hare, badger and the now rare otter. Water voles, water shrews and the harmless grass snake enjoy a dip in search of prey. The grass snake, which can grow over one metre in length, is an excellent swimmer.

Kingfishers, grey wagtails, mute swans, reed warblers and colourful dragonflies – green, purple, bronze – all frequent rivers.

BROWN HARE

OTTER

FOX

BADGER

WATER VOLE

WATER SHREW

39. Animals of woodland and fresh water, and their tracks.

13

LAKES, LOCHS AND RESERVOIRS

40. Loch Leven.

Lakes are large areas of water, surrounded by land. A loch is a Scottish lake; "sea lochs" connect with the sea. A lough is an Irish lake.

Reservoirs are man-made lakes. They collect, store and pipe our tap water. Reservoirs are created by damming and flooding a valley; or gouged out of the earth and filled with water.

Lake Windermere, in England's Lake District, is 17km long. Loch Lomond is 39km in length and the largest area of freshwater in Britain; in parts Loch Lomond is 190m deep. Loch Morar is the deepest loch in Britain (310m).

Fish like light, well-oxygenated upper levels of water, and seldom descend into dark, oxygen-thin depths below 13m.

FASCINATING FACTS
Imprisoned for over 10,000 years! The ancient and at one time migratory Char *(Salvelinus alpinus)* has been cut off

from the sea since the land upheavals of the last Ice Age trapped their spawning ancestors in a smattering of deep cold water lakes in England (notably Lake Windermere), Wales, Scotland and Ireland.

41. Char.

Char live far down in icy waters, and are rarely fished for by anglers; though they can be caught by deep trolling (see page 29) or spinning. Big char weigh 340g or above. The average char weighs about 225g. This beautiful and mysterious species is a member of the Salmon family, resembles the trout in shape; is much brighter in colour: purple-blue back; golden eyes; scarlet, gold-tinted sides, with flashes of yellow. Body dotted with pink, orange and white spots.

Lakes, Scottish lochs and Irish loughs hide monster fish of several species, especially trout, perch, pike and eels. The most fearsome giant of the depths is the pike. Lochs could prove the key to record-breaking success.

A pike 7 feet (2.13m) in length, weighing 72 lbs (32.65kg) was caught on Loch Ken by John Murray in 1774. The jaws (recently checked) measure 153mm wide, with sharp teeth 26mm long! The pike was old and malnourished when captured. In peak condition it probably topped 45kg! A pike of 90 lbs 8 oz (41kg) was reported landed from Ireland's

Lough Derg, in 1862. John Garvin caught a pike in Lough Conn, 1920 weighed at 53 lbs (24kg). Tommy Morgan landed a pike of 47 lbs 11 oz (21kg) from Loch Lomond in 1945.

TIP

To catch a monster pike, and steal the rod-caught record: First, pick a likely loch; bait a big sea fishing hook (6/0) with a fresh 1½–2kg trout (preferably sea trout); attach one metre of high breaking-strain (27kg) wire trace, to about 275m of extra-strong line (11kg). Use powerful tackle, and have ready a long-handled sea gaff landing hook. Be careful, a *monster* pike will easily bite off your arm. Good hunting!

Lake, loch and reservoir fish
Lakes: Bream, carp, char (rare), eel, perch, pike, roach, rudd, tench, brown trout, rainbow trout (occasionally). A few lakes hold zander. Sea trout and salmon enter some lakes at spawning time.
Lochs: Perch, pike, eel, char (rare), brown trout, sea trout, salmon.
Reservoirs: Bream, carp, eel, perch, pike, roach, rudd, tench, brown trout, rainbow trout.

42. Rainbow Trout.

Right lake, loch and reservoir methods include: Float fishing; fly fishing; free-lining; legering; paternostering; spinning; trolling.

Great spots to fish

*Let fishes show you the great spots to fish. Don polarised sun-glasses; scan and *listen* across and into the water for fish and signs of feeding; rings, ripples, splashes and waves caused by surface-feeding fish; shoals of terrified fry scattering from predators; misty swirls of disturbed sediment; tugged weeds/plants; bubbles breaking the surface etc.

*Beneath overhanging trees or shrubs.

*In deep water near the mouth of inflowing streams.

*Channels around small islands, especially any deep holes or gullies and patches of water beneath island tree branches or bushy shrubs.

*Near newly collapsed bankside.

*Recently flooded ground; particularly ditches, semi-submerged posts, bushes etc.

*Ambush stations occupied by predatory fish: heavy reed/weed areas; hollows, deep holes and channels near the shore.

*During cold or changeable weather, expect fish to be feeding well beneath the surface (2m to 7m) in deep water, away from the shore. Freezing winter weather may force big fish down 13m from the surface.

*Warm weather draws fish into the upper water level (3m); the surface, and water's edge shallows.

Summer: stretches of shallow water shaded from strong sunlight.

*Deep water next to shallow areas where insects hatch and fish fry play.

*On windy days fish with the wind blowing from behind you. Fishes gather near shallows to feast on insects blown from land into the water. When the wind has ceased, try the opposite shore for bonus catches.

*Observe where wind-caused currents and cross-currents carry particles of food to queueing fish; cast into the current and wait for a bite!

*Cast to the point where rippling wind-driven water meets

calm stretches protected by shore contours and/or vegetation.

*Fish methodically along the line of rippling water – which traps and whirls food to waiting fishes.

*Strong gusty winds or squalls send fish deep and into sheltered bays. Quiet, wind-protected spots may offer good sport.

*On cloudy, overcast, rainy days, excellent catches can be enjoyed *before* and *after* rain. Fish swim deep and take a break whilst rain teems into the water.

43. Mountain lough in County Kerry.

Lake, loch and reservoir success hints
1. Check if a detailed map of the water you intend fishing is marketed by the water authority/owner, and buy one. The information marked shows obvious "hotspots", and the map is convenient for recording your own secret finds!
2. Although fish in lakes, lochs and reservoirs rove widely in search of food, individual fishes and shoals still have favourite feeding spots, and sometimes become slaves to

habit. Careful observation can suggest suitable timing for a shrewdly calculated catch.

3. Watch for patches of shore scoured or worn bare by anglers' boots. Popular places may have much to recommend them, though not always.

4. Try not to be framed from behind by sunlight. Apart from the fish-warning silhouette and shadow, your rod and line will flash clear warning signals through the water.

5. Lake, loch and reservoir big fish, generally like to have their main meals at dawn, dusk and into the night. At these times they feel safe and are therefore most vulnerable.

6. A spell of settled weather suits the fish. Good catches are practically certain when there's a steady south-westerly breeze on a dull day. Hot, sunny, clear-sky days produce poor results, though night fishing may score fine catches. Wind and rain after a scorching near-drought period often brings spectacular results!

7. Moonless, mild nights yield large catches.

8. Big fish may follow your bait for a while before striking. Be patient.

9. Take depth temperature readings with an angler's special thermometer (see page 28) and record them in your notebook, alongside a report of the day's sport. A correlation between water temperatures and catches will reward you with the information necessary to predict accurately bumper bags of big fish, and be the toast of your friends.

TACKLE + TIPS

In addition to the main items of tackle recommended in Chapter 4, you may find some of these extras worth buying or saving-up for.

● Take a set of heavy duty waterproofs when fishing the exposed, weather-changeable, wild waters of lakes, lochs and reservoirs. Cutting winds chill the body to freezing; sheets of bullet rain gun through flimsy garments. Make sure there's a large hood to pull over your *woolly hat*.

● A long scarf stops icy wind funnelling down your neck.

● Anglers' lightweight rough weather shelters – compact tent type, or speedily erected anglers' umbrella-style wrap around shelters, protect 2 anglers from hostile weather. A

44. Steep hills surrounding Loch Skene.

godsend if you're pinned down in an isolated place, or
determined to fish come hell or high water, and land the
monster you know is out there . . .
● Insect repellent deters wee winged beasties from eating you
alive. Small midges bite big on large waters.

Lake, loch and reservoir nature trail
A marvellous opportunity to study the multitude of water
fowl who reside on or visit large expanses of still water: coot,
tufted duck, mallard, heron, mute swan, cormorant,
widgeon, teal, pochard, black-headed gull, moorhen,
dabchick, herring gull, great crested grebe etc.

14

WEATHER LORE

The ancient country tradition of forecasting weather according to nature's signs often rewards us with correct predictions. We should not ignore old wisdom passed down through the ages. Mother Nature's sign language is rich, varied and easy to understand. Listen to Her and know whether to expect rain or shine, and when to go fishing with nature's guarantee of good sport!

Natural barometers
Pine cones, kept in a shaded place away from sunlight and direct heat, open when fine weather is expected and close if wet or unsettled weather is approaching.

Seaweed, rinsed in cold water, allowed to dry naturally and hung somewhere away from sunlight and direct heat, is dry and brittle before fine weather; becoming more loose, flexible, shiny and life-like when rain or unsettled weather is due. "Sea belt" *(Laminaria saccharina)* seaweed makes an especially effective weather forecaster.

Anglers' wise sayings
The sage advice, detailed below, is taken from my angling notebook. Frequently, the wisdom of the sayings is proven; occasionally the advice is poor, or incorrect. Your confidence, skill and determination may catch fish, even when country wisdom is set against you.

"Red sky at night, anglers' delight. Get there early – give the fish a fight!" Make an early morning (dawn) start. At first pay special attention to water near the bankside, then try deep stretches and pools. Sport is likely to tail off before midday; then pick up early evening and continue to dusk.

"Grey mist at dawn, fish biting at dusk and early morn." Dawn low mist is a good sign. Fish begin feeding at first light, speed their search for food as the water warms and may continue biting until mid-morning. After digesting break-

fast, the fish dine again late evening, as daylight fades.

"Dew on grass at night, go fishing at first light." Rise early; be at the waterside for daybreak and enjoy great sport. Many fish feed ravenously in bankside shallows and at the surface; dropping deeper as the day wears on.

"Rain before seven, fat fish by eleven!" Early morning rain means big catches. Sometimes during, but especially after, a heavy downpour, fish feed voraciously at all levels in the muddied water; maybe continuing into early afternoon.

Changes

Sudden or sharp changes in weather unsettle fish; feeding patterns become erratic and difficult to predict. Breaking weather is heralded by changes in temperature, wind, clouds and visibility.

Wind direction

"Coming from the North or East, catches least." A strong north or east wind can discourage fish from feeding, and results may be poor, though big fish can still be caught by the wily angler.

"Blowing from the South or West bags biggest and best." The south and west winds are the fishes' friends and anglers' ally. Fish feed with gusto, and bonus catches are probable.

Moon and stars

"On dark, cloudy, moonless nights, the angler high should set his sights." Expect good night-time catches of big fish when the night is black, particularly when the air is warm.

"Bright, cloudless, moonlit nights, always give fishes the frights." Night fishing may be poor on quiet waters bathed in revealing moonlight. Fish seem nervous of feeding, and acutely sensitive to the slightest noise or vibration; spooked by anglers' moving shadows, and uneasy until daybreak, when they breakfast.

A clear, silver-white moon and bright stars foretell a fine day. The fewer stars, the better the day.

When the moon looks pale and stars unclear, or the moon is ringed by a shimmering halo, expect rain.

Wildlife
All creatures and plants respond to clear signals they receive about coming changes in weather. When we learn to recognise the different responses, we too, can predict the weather to come. Among my favourite natural weather indicators, are gnats and crows.

Gnats
When early morning gnats cloud in the open, the day will be sunny.

Crows
Persistent croaking by one or more crows means rain. Aerobatic wheeling and diving of crows is a sign of strong winds and bad weather to come... pack waterproofs, and be prepared to hang on to your hat!

45. Hooded Crow.

15

HOW TO KEEP A NOTEBOOK

Detailed angling records help us hook prize catches of specimen-size fish. Each species of fish responds to our baits and style of presentation in a unique way. The type of natural food favoured by particular species of fish changes with the year's seasons; varies from one water to another, and our baits must keep pace with the feeding whims of hook-shy fish who've learned to recognise and reject anglers' popular baits that have been over-fished in the past.

Modern research suggests fish learn from their mistakes; some species of fish have demonstrated a relatively high level of cleverness, cunning, and possibly intuitive awareness of predators, including anglers!

To win consistently in our battle of wits with large fish (who live to grow big by being smart) we must keep accurate records and learn from our success and blunders.

Your fishing notebook is an essential aid to better freshwater fishing and sea angling results.

Angling progress comes after observation; careful thought and constant experiment with new and original methods, baits and tackle.

Making notes

During, or immediately after, your fishing expedition, write on a fresh page: the *date* and *place* visited; *weather conditions* – you may include air temperature and wind direction; *state of water* – depth, clear or murky; fast flowing, slow or still; water temperature etc.

Jot down the *time* you catch the fish and *identify the species*.

Describe the *location* and/or *position* in the water where the fish took your bait (below overhanging shrub; mid-water depth; on the bottom etc.) and the type of bait or artificial fly used.

Note and/or draw the arrangement of hook, weights (if

any) and float (if any) that brought success. You might like to comment on the performance of rod, reel or line.

Enter the species of the *best fish* of the outing; its approximate or measured *size:* length (from nose/snout tip to inner "V" of tail fork) and maximum width (from belly to back) and if you like, *weight* (using an angler's weigh-net, suspended from an accurate spring-balance).

Write down any *remarks* you may want to make about the fish (condition; strength; sporting quality; time fish took to recover and swim away after release etc.), or other details of the day's events.

DATE & TIME	ROUTE	WEATHER	OBSERVATIONS
27 June 07.30hrs to 11.30hrs	Across forest heath; along woodland track to stony bank at edge of the deep pool of the trout stream.	Bright and fine (25°C). Blue sky; some high whispy cirrus clouds.	**HEATH** Gorse bushes flowering rich yellow; Bell Heather purple; Sheep's Sorrel (30 cm high). **WOOD** Heard drumming on tree and saw Great-Spotted Woodpecker! Rabbit (many fresh droppings); Grey Squirrels. Clear prints of Fox in soft earth. Honeysuckle (fragrant scent); Pinky Foxgloves (1m high). **STREAM** Red Deer (5) drinking! Saw Water Shrew; Kingfisher flashed past! Brown Trout rising to seize midges.

46. Notebook: Nature trail.

Finally, note interesting observations of *wildlife:* animals, birds, plants, insects etc.

The more detailed and complete your records, the more you learn about the behaviour of fish; catches will improve and increase with your knowledge, and the fact-packed notebook will soon be worth its weight in gold!

Wildlife and nature page

All sorts of valuable information can be included in your notebook. Separate pages may be devoted to special interests you combine with angling. For instance, it's fun to take a few pocket-sized, illustrated identification guides, and write a Nature Trail Page, highlighting sightings made while rambling to and from the waterside on a fishing trip.

Maps

Sketched maps of each water visited, indicating precise places where fish have been caught – by yourself, or others, are a great help (see examples on pages 48, 54, and 72). I often pencil positions of fish spotted and places I'd expect to catch particular species.

Charts

Construct charts in your notebook, at the close of each fishing season, to pin-point the fish-catching effectiveness of baits and artificial flies (see examples on pages 36, 43 and 109). Charts are easily referred to, and offer instant access to important information vital to fishing success.

Charts and *graphs* can be drawn to show much valuable angling information. Many important facts only become clear when displayed visually on a chart or graph.

16

CONSERVING THE FRESHWATER ENVIRONMENT

To preserve the life and continued existence of fish, aquatic creatures, plants and animals of freshwater and the waterside – we must act now!

Man is upsetting the perfect harmony of Nature. Ponds are being infilled; marshes drained; fertilisers and pesticides soak through soil into freshwater and poison life; discharged industrial waste and oil leaks pollute and kill.

Many species may die unless we help them today (the otter is in danger; frogs and toads are threatened); some water life has recently become extinct (including several species of dragonfly).

47. A beautiful Broads scene.

Pollution, wave action and water bottom disturbance caused by busy holiday boat traffic on the beautiful Norfolk Broads, have led to the death of plants, fish and animals. Increasing recreational boat traffic poses a serious threat to life on numerous waters.

We *share* this planet with myriad life forms. Humans are only one thread woven into Nature's complex and delicate web of life. When any species becomes extinct, a single thread is cut and the whole web trembles and is affected. We cannot survive apart from Nature, because we are *part* of Nature. Conservation concerns us, and is ultimately vital to the survival of the human species.

What we can do

1. Join the nearest *angling club*, and actively assist the club's carefully planned and co-ordinated efforts to clear polluted local waters and keep all water life strong and healthy.

2. Join the *Anglers' Co-operative Association.* Your tiny membership fee helps the A.C.A. win battles against pollution on our behalf. Ask your tackle dealer for a membership form, or the address to write for one.

3. Shut gates; leave flowers untrampled; animals and birds undisturbed.

4. Gently return caught fish to their water with a minimum of handling.

5. Gather and bin any fishing line, hooks or weights we find littering the waterside – left by ignorant anglers.

Garden ponds

Ready-moulded garden ponds or pond liners are available in sizes to suit most gardens, look beautiful, are ideal homes for attractive resident fish and water plants; encourage many species of wildlife, and bring the magic sounds and sights of the countryside into an otherwise ordinary garden.

Ponds give us the opportunity to study fish behaviour, feeding times, preferred natural food, and reaction to small samples of "secret" groundbait recipes. My pond fish go wild with joy when fed titbits of crumbled shortbread, chocolate cake, or cold porridge!

TIP

Pet pond fish furnish us with many clues to improve our fishing technique.

17

SEA FISHING

Sea fishing, is the exhilarating sport of angling for fish that live in salt water of the sea, and mixed salt and fresh (*brackish*) water of river-mouth estuaries.

No rod licence or fishing permit is normally needed to fish in the sea, though some piers require you to buy an inexpensive pier fishing ticket. And there is no close season for sea angling.

Tides
Most coastal areas have two high tides, and two low tides in a period of 24 hours. A high tide is an incoming and steadily rising *flood* tide, that flows over beaches and into estuaries until it reaches a reasonably predictable high water level (high tide), before the tide turns and begins to flow (*ebb*) back out to sea until the water reaches a specially low level (low tide). After a brief pause, the pattern is repeated. The times of high and low water are printed in angling weekly newspapers; sea angling magazines; local newspapers, and are, of course, known to our friend – the local fishing tackle dealer.

Fish shoal movements
To keep up-to-date with the movements and present position of travelling fish shoals, and the currently successful fish-catching baits, read the sea angling press; angling news columns in the local newspaper; chat with tackle dealers and sea anglers.

Sea Angling Club
The best and quickest way to become a wise and proficient sea angler, is to join a sea angling club. Some freshwater fishing clubs also take members sea fishing. Club anglers have the chance to enjoy the adventure and thrills of boat angling at sea, under the experienced and expert guidance of a professional charter boat skipper.

Knots

The tucked half blood knot (see page 8) is usually adequate for sea fishing. The **palomar knot** (see fig 48, below) is a slightly stronger knot, preferred by many sea anglers for tying line to hooks and/or swivels.

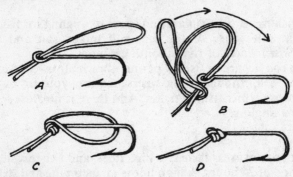

48. Palomar knot.

Dangerous fish

Watch out for poisonous weevers! The tiny Lesser Weever *(Trachinus vipera)* lives half-buried in sand beneath shallow water. Spines of the first dorsal fin and gill covers can inject poison when touched. The poison causes rapid and painful swelling. Go straight to the nearest doctor or hospital if stung by a weever.

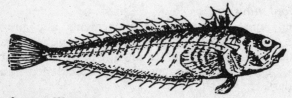

49. Lesser Weever.

Description: Drab yellow/brown body (about 150mm long). First dorsal fin black.

You may hook a Sting Ray *(Dasyatis pastinaca)*. The sting ray is found mainly in southern waters – summer and autumn, and sometimes feeds close inshore. The sting ray's tail is armed with one (occasionally two!!) arrow-like and venom-injecting spine(s). These spines can cause very nasty wounds. When you see you've hooked a sting ray, carefully cut your fishing line and let the fish swim away. If you're stung by the sting ray's spine(s) go immediately to the nearest doctor or hospital (preferably hospital).

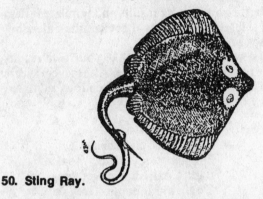

50. Sting Ray.

Description: Brown-grey back; grey-white underneath. The average sting ray weighs round 7kg.

Safety kit
Carry a safety kit comprising of (at least): first aid plasters (assorted sizes); roll of bandage; antiseptic cream; a whistle to attract attention should you need help; a torch.

Safety notes
Care is necessary near slippery rocks and deep water. Be aware of dangerous quicksands and treacherous mud-flats – keep clear of them! Learn to swim, and always go fishing with a friend. Tell someone where you intend fishing and what time to expect you back.

Be sensible and stay safe.

Conservation
Release straightway and unharmed, all small sea fish caught, and large fish not wanted for bait or cooking. Collect left-over snippets and lengths of line. Check no hooks or weights are left lying about. Take litter home, and dispose of it there. Thank you.

18

FISH

I've sorted my best shore fishing results and tabulated them in the form of a calendar. I find this "Best Results Calendar" helpful, and hope you do too.

At the end of a year's sea fishing, make your own results calendar and see how it differs from mine. After several years your calendar will be complete, and a tremendous aid to sea angling success.

Shore Angling Best Results Calendar

Mid-April	— Bass/Coalfish/Conger Eel/ Dogfish/Grey Mullet/Plaice.
May	— Bass/Coalfish/Conger Eel/Dab/ Dogfish/Flounder/Grey Mullet/ Plaice/Pollack/Wrasse.
June	— Bass/Coalfish/Conger Eel/Dab/ Dogfish/Flounder/Mackerel/Grey Mullet/Plaice/Pollack/Pouting/ Sole/Wrasse.
July	— Bass/Coalfish/Conger Eel/Dab/ Dogfish/Flounder/Mackerel/Grey Mullet/Plaice/Pollack/Pouting/ Sole/Wrasse.
August	— Bass/Coalfish/Conger Eel/Dab/ Dogfish/Flounder/Mackerel/Grey Mullet/Plaice/Pollack/Pouting/ Sole/Wrasse.
September	— Bass/Coalfish/Cod/Conger Eel/ Dab/Dogfish/Flounder/Mackerel/ Grey Mullet/Plaice/Pollack/ Pouting/Sole/Wrasse.
October	— Bass/Coalfish/Cod/Conger Eel/ Dab/Dogfish/Flounder/Grey Mullet/Plaice/Pollack/Pouting/ Whiting/Wrasse.
November	— Coalfish/Cod/Conger Eel/Dab/ Flounder/Whiting.

December	— Cod/Dab/Flounder/Whiting.
January	— Cod/Dab/Whiting.
February	— Cod/Dab/Whiting.
March – mid-April	— Blank.

As you see, I begin sea fishing from the shore (beaches, rocks, harbours, estuaries, piers) round mid-April and carry on to the end of February. I take a 6 or 7 week break from shore fishing between March and mid-April because, although sea fish can still be caught from the shore, catches are uncertain and sport generally sparse. Many species of fish are in deep offshore water, beyond the reach of shore anglers, or returning from distant feeding and spawning grounds.

Bass *(Dicentrachus labrax).*
Preferred locations: Bass love rough water and fast currents, over any type of seabed. Bass can be caught from shore, harbour, pier or estuary.
Popular angling methods: Paternostering; legering; driftlining; float fishing; spinning.
Note: Be aware of sharp spines at the front of the bass's dorsal fin. Some sea anglers wear a thick leather glove to lift bass from the water.

TIPS
Fishing for bass is best when incoming rising *(flood)* tide waves break into surf and white water. Bass feed in the turbulent and tumbling foam. The peak of high tide fishes well, as do the first 2 hours of the outflowing *(ebb)* tide. For several days after a gale, bass offer excellent sport. On calm, clear days, reasonable catches may be achieved at dusk and after dark.
    Bass feed at all depths. If in doubt about the right depth to float fish – try mid-water level.

Coalfish *(Pollachius virens).*
Preferred locations: Rocky shores and rock-strewn rough seabed; also harbours, piers and estuaries.
Popular angling methods: Float fishing; driftlining; spinning.

TIPS
Coalfish feed along the water bottom during the day, but

may be caught at dawn/early morning and dusk/evening at mid-water depth; also close to and at, the water surface.

Cod *(Gadus morhua).*
Preferred locations: Deep water over most types of seabed, particularly patches of sand or sand/mud and weed-covered rocks. Good catches of cod can be made from deep water off steep sloping shores; also from piers and the mouths of estuaries.
Popular angling methods: Legering; paternostering.

TIPS
Big cod gulp *big* baits, so don't be shy – load a large hook with a bumper portion of bait. Present your hookbait on, or near, the water bottom.

Conger Eel *(Conger conger).*
Preferred locations: Rocky seabed; crevices between rocks; holes and cracks in harbour walls; beneath piers and in estuaries (near rocks, rough ground, posts, sunken debris etc).
Popular angling methods: Legering; paternostering.
Notes: Conger eels have sharp teeth which may sever fishing line. Tie an angler's *wire conger trace* between hook and main line when angling for large conger eels. Conger eels can stay alive and *give a nasty bite,* long after being removed from water. The only certain way to kill congers wanted for cooking, is to cut through the backbone with an angler's *sharp* filleting knife.

TIPS
"Small" conger eels, up to 4kg in weight, may feed in daylight. Many conger eels, including the BIG monster congers, track food at dusk and after dark. Conger eels like to feed in settled weather, but amazingly good sport can be enjoyed when there's "thunder in the air", before a storm. Conger eels scent their prey, so use whole fresh fish (mackerel, herring etc.) or fillets, strips or chunks of fresh fish as bait. Present your hookbait on, or near, the water bottom.

Dab *(Limanda limanda).*
Preferred locations: Sandy seabed; also piers and sand/mud

estuaries.
Popular angling methods: Legering; paternostering.

TIPS
Dabs feed on, or close to, the water bottom. They seize bait
that shows movement, so raise and lower your rod tip
occasionally and/or reel-in, and then release a little line, to
give your hookbait an extra-lively look and enhanced dab-
appeal.

Dogfish
Five species of dogfish are commonly caught round our
shores, from beaches, rocks and piers.
Smoothhound *(Mustelus mustelus)*.
Starry Smoothhound *(Mustelus asterias)*.
Bull Huss *(Scyliorhinus stellaris)*.
Lesser Spotted Dogfish *(Scyliorhinus canicula)*.
Spurdog *(Squalus acanthias)*.
Preferred locations: Smoothhounds, starry smoothhounds
and lesser spotted dogfish, like sandy and sand/mud areas of
seabed. Bull huss prefer a rocky, rough bottom. Spurdogs
can turn up anywhere!
Popular angling methods: Legering.
Note: Bull huss and lesser spotted dogfish have rough skin.
Handle them firmly and with caution. Some sea anglers wear
a thick leather glove to grip bull huss and lesser spotted
dogfish.
    The spurdog has 2 sharp spines *(spurs)*, one at the front of
each of the 2 dorsal fins. Watch for these spines, and don't let
this "dog" spur you!

TIPS
Smoothhounds, starry smoothhounds, bull huss and lesser
spotted dogfish feed mainly along the seabed. Spurdogs feed
at any depth from seabed to water surface.
    Smoothhounds and starry smoothhounds are the dogfish
popularly pursued by sea anglers. The other dogfish species
are not often deliberately fished for; though when cooked,
all dogfish taste delicious!
    When fishing for any species of dogfish, it's wise to tie an
angler's *wire trace* between hook and main line; dogfish teeth
may grind through normal strength fishing line. Some sea

anglers prefer to use a 1.5m trace cut from extra-strong
fishing line, of about 22.68kg (50 lb) breaking strain.

Flounder *(Platichthys flesus).*
Preferred locations: Sandy and muddy seabed; harbours
and piers; also estuaries and often well up river.
Popular angling methods: Legering; paternostering; float
fishing; driftlining; spinning.

TIPS
Flounders like to lie at the bottom of gullies, hollows and
seabed depressions. They grab food swept over them by the
current. Present your hookbait on, or near, the water
bottom. Flounders pursue lively-looking baits. An occasionally jerked rod tip; reeling-in and release of about a metre of
line etc., excites flounders into chasing and seizing the
hookbait.

Mackerel *(Scomber scombrus).*
Preferred locations: Mackerel shoals feed over all types of
seabed; are caught from beaches, rocks, piers, harbours;
sometimes shoals enter estuaries and swim up river.
Popular angling methods: Float fishing; driftlining;
spinning.

TIPS
A rising tide in warm, settled weather, carries mackerel
shoals close inshore. A warm evening high tide can produce
bags of caught mackerel, sufficient to deep freeze and supply
you with bait and the family with cooked fish dishes, for
weeks!
    Mackerel feed at varying water depths; for best results
present your hookbait near the surface. Large mackerel can
often be caught at mid-water depth.

Thick-lipped **Grey Mullet** *(Chelon labrosus).*
    And thin-lipped grey mullet *(Liza ramada).*
Preferred locations: Sandy and muddy shores; piers,
harbours and estuaries.
Popular angling methods: Float fishing; driftlining; paternostering; legering; spinning.

TIPS

Grey mullet feed at all depths, from water bottom to water surface. Feeding mullet forage through thick weed on stones, rocks, harbour walls and pier or jetty supports. The best time to fish for mullet is at dawn and *early* morning on a rising *(flood)* tide. Mullet seldom feed at dusk or after dark.

Estuary feeding mullet respond favourably to freshwater baits (see Chapter 6); mullet favourites include: bread, cheese, maggots, earthworms.

Plaice *(Pleuronectes platessa).*
Preferred locations: Sandy/muddy shores; also harbours and estuaries.
Popular angling methods: Legering; paternostering; drift-lining (deep).

TIPS

Calm water, a few hours before dusk, yields good catches of plaice. Present your hookbait on, or near, the water bottom. Plaice may rise to mid-water depth to seize an especially appetising and well presented bait.

Pollack *(Pollachius pollachius).*
Preferred locations: Rocky areas and inshore reefs; also caught from harbours and piers.
Popular angling methods: Legering; spinning; float fishing; driftlining.

TIPS

At dawn and dusk, pollack may feed at, or near, the water surface. During daytime pollack feed along the water bottom. Round and above weed-covered seabed rocks, is a favourite pollack haunt.

Pouting *(Trisopterus luscus).*
Preferred locations: Rough, sand-grit seabed; rocky shores; also caught from harbours and piers.
Popular angling methods: Legering; paternostering; float fishing.

TIPS

Pouting feed keenly at the peak of high tide, particularly late afternoon and evening. Big catches are probable about dusk and after dark. Pouting feed on, or near, the water bottom, and rise to feed at mid-water depth.

Sole *(Solea solea).*
Preferred locations: Sandy and muddy seabed; patches of sand/mud between rocks.
Popular angling methods: Legering; paternostering; drift-lining (deep).

TIPS
Best sport after dark on a rising *(flood)* tide. Present hookbait on, or close to, the water bottom.

Whiting *(Merlangius merlangus).*
Preferred locations: Sandy and muddy seabed; also caught from rocky shores and piers.
Popular angling methods: Paternostering; driftlining.

TIPS
Expect good catches of whiting round dusk and after dark, near peak of high tide; also as the tide turns to ebb. Present your hookbait on, or near, the water bottom, or at mid-water depth.

Ballan Wrasse *(Labrus bergylta).*
Preferred locations: Rocky shores and rocky rough seabed; also sandy areas between rocks, and by harbour walls.
Popular angling methods: Float fishing; paternostering; legering.

TIPS
Wrasse eat rock-clinging creatures, and feed close to the rock face. A rising *(flood)* tide gives great sport. Present your hookbait approximately 350mm above the seabed for best results.
All ballan wrasse are born female. After about 9 years some female wrasse change into males. Ballan wrasse can live over 20 years. At breeding time, female ballan wrasse build nests of seaweed to lay their eggs in.

19

TACKLE

At a pinch, you can use strong freshwater tackle (see Chapter 4) to fish from harbour walls, jetties, estuaries, rocks and piers. To cast a long distance from the beach, you'll need a *beachcaster* sea fishing rod, although I've used a powerful freshwater rod to *driftline* successfully (see page 101) from beaches for flounders, bass, dabs and grey mullet.

Suitable specialist sea fishing tackle for different techniques of sea angling is recommended in the "Tackle + Tips" sections of Chapters 22 to 25.

TIPS
Always consult your tackle dealer before buying important items of sea fishing tackle. Correctly balanced equipment is vital to achieve optimum angling performance. Improperly matched tackle is a waste of your money. It pays to ask before you buy!

List of essential tackle
Rod – a beachcaster rod of about 3.35m (11 feet) in length is a good first buy for the beginner, and is satisfactory for all-round sea angling from the shore (beach, rocks, pier, harbour wall, jetty, estuary).
Reel – fixed-spool sea reel for general shore angling.
Line – always fill the reel to maximum capacity with quality line. See the "Tackle + Tips" section of Chapters 22 to 25 for suggested line strengths.
Hooks – top quality, *sharp* hooks; a selection of sizes (see Hook Tips on page 108) including: sizes 6, 2, 1/0, 3/0 and/or 4/0.
Weights – torpedo, pear, ball, bomb and barrel shape weights are best. Weights with attached wires are designed to grip the seabed in strong currents. Weights without wires work well for all-round shore angling. I advise beginners to

start sea fishing with weights ranging from 14g (½ oz) to 85g (3 oz).

TIPS
Always choose the smallest weight required to cast your line to the place you expect fish to be feeding, and heavy enough to hold your hookbait in position long enough to attract a bite!
Floats – freshwater floats (see page 24) can be used when fishing small baits in calm water. Special sea floats are marketed for presenting large baits to big fish in rough and deep water.

Important additional items of tackle
*Articles marked with an asterisk * are also recommended in Chapter 4 and may be used for freshwater fishing and sea fishing.
Rod bag, to store and protect your sea rod.
Reel case, to store and protect your sea reel.
**Hook sharpener*, to hone hooks sharp.
**Bait boxes* – separate boxes for different baits.
**Artery forceps* or sea hook disgorger to remove your hook safely from the fish's mouth.
Sea angler's drop net, to land hooked heavy fish that might break your line if lifted from the water. The drop net ties to strong cord and is lowered over pier, jetty, harbour wall or rocks, and under the hooked big fish. Your netted fish is then raised and landed.
A * *long-handled large landing net* does the same job in estuaries and from low jetties.
Sea angler's sharp filleting knife, to cut bait or gut and fillet caught fish wanted for bait or cooking.
Bait cutting board, on which to hold bait safely and securely for cutting.
Strong, thin-bladed pocket knife, to prise open, and scoop out shellfish for bait.
   Saltwater corrodes tackle. Wash all tackle used for sea fishing in cold tap water at home, before drying and storing.

20

METHODS

Driftlining

Aim: To release fishing line steadily, and allow the hookbait to drift naturally with the current towards feeding fish.

Driftlining is a similar method to freshwater "free-lining" (see page 26).

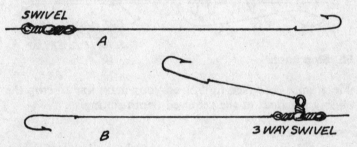

51. Driftlines.

Rig: Driftline rigs may be fished with one or 2 baited hooks (see fig 51). In rigs "A" and "B" allow about 1½m between the hook at the end of your main line and swivel. With rig "B" the distance between second hook and 3 way swivel, should be at least 305mm.

TIPS

Attach little, if any, weight to the line. Driftline in places where your line won't snag on submerged obstacles. Gradually let out line from your reel, to a maximum length of roughly 20m. Occasionally reel-in and then release a metre or two of line; this action raises and waves your hookbait enticingly in the water.

Float fishing

The *aims* of float fishing are broadly the same as in

freshwater float fishing (see page 24). And freshwater floats may be used when sea angling with a small bait in calm water. However, in choppy or rough water; when presenting your float-fished hookbait deeper than 2m, or fishing a heavy bait – use an angler's *sliding sea float*.

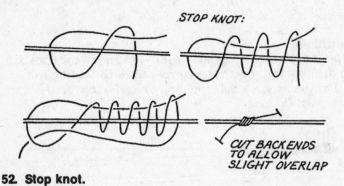

STOP KNOT:

CUT BACK ENDS
TO ALLOW
SLIGHT OVERLAP

52. Stop knot.

Tie a *stop knot* (see fig 52) on your main line to stop the sliding sea float at the required depth-setting.

TIP
Raise or lower, where necessary, your float's depth-setting to allow for rise or fall in water depth due to tide change (high tide – low tide).

Groundbaiting
The *aim* of groundbaiting and "feeding" is the same as described for freshwater fishing (see page 26). Because tidal currents may carry groundbait and loose feed far from the spot being fished, many sea anglers use a fine-mesh net bag – stuffed with groundbait mix, and lowered beneath the water on a length of strong cord. The scent soon brings shoals of feeding fish to the net bag – nearby is your hook, baited with a sumptuous and irresistible bait!

TIP
Prepare at least 680g of groundbait for your net bag. Fresh, chopped, oily fish (herring, mackerel, sprat, pilchard) is best. Crushed shellfish (mussels, limpets etc.) are effective. Add

some bran/stale bread crumbs, and a liberal squeeze of angler's pilchard oil.

I know "cheats" who simply use shop-bought meaty dog or cat food. It works reasonably well. Does dog food groundbait attract dogfish? Yes, it does!

Legering

The *aim* of legering is the same as freshwater legering (see page 27).

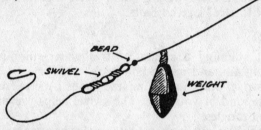

53. Basic leger rig.

Rig: The main line is free to run through the leger weight's eye, and fish won't feel the weight's resistance before biting your baited hook. A sea angling *bead* on the line between swivel and weight protects your knot from the mobile weight's weakening wear. The distance between hook and swivel should be at least 305mm.

Paternostering

Aims: To present hookbait in a stationary position above the water bottom.

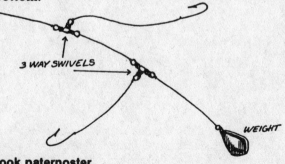

54. 2 hook paternoster.

Rig: Two hooks may be attached to the rig (see fig 54) and fish offered 2 alternative baits at different depths. The distance between swivels, and swivel and weight, is variable, but should normally be about 460mm. Each hook should be approximately 205mm from the swivel.

TIP

The paternoster is a convenient and effective rig when fishing crab-infested water, where bottom-scouring crabs are quick to steal legered baits.

Spinning

Saltwater spinning is similar to freshwater spinning (see page 29) in aim and method.

Tie a swivel onto the fishing line about 1 metre from the lure at the end of your line. The swivel helps prevent line twists and tangles.

A sea angling *anti-kink weight* can also be attached on the line to sink your lure deep in the water, slow the rate of spin, and further reduce risk of line twist and kinks.

Jigging: Method of presenting and fishing a bait (often an artificial lure). The line is cast and bait/lure slowly reeled-in; an unsteady "jerked" motion is imparted to the bait/lure by raising and lowering your rod tip, and reeling-in at varied speeds. *Pirk* lures are jigged.

21

BAITS

Hungry sea fish will snatch any edible creature properly presented as hookbait. However, many species of sea fish have favourite natural foods, and show a preference for particular baits. Here's a basic guide to some successful fish-catching baits:

Sea Fishing Bait Guide

Bait	*Fish*
Clam	— Bass/Cod/Dogfish/Flounder/Plaice/ Sole/Wrasse.
Cockle	— Bass/Coalfish/Cod/Dab/Dogfish/ Flounder/Plaice/Pollack/Pouting/Sole/ Whiting/Wrasse.
Crab	— Bass/Cod/Conger Eel/Dab/Dogfish/ Flounder/Grey Mullet/Plaice/Pollack/ Pouting/Sole/Whiting/Wrasse.
Fresh Fish	— Bass/Coalfish/Cod/Conger Eel/Dab/ Dogfish/Flounder/Mackerel/Grey Mullet/Pollack/Pouting/Sole/Whiting/ Wrasse.
Lugworm	— Bass/Coalfish/Cod/Conger Eel/Dab/ Dogfish/Flounder/Plaice/Pouting/Sole/ Whiting/Wrasse.
Lure	— Bass/Coalfish/Cod/Flounder/Mackerel/ Grey Mullet/Pollack/Whiting.
Mussel	— Bass/Coalfish/Cod/Dab/Flounder/ Mackerel/Grey Mullet/Plaice/Pollack/ Pouting/Sole/Whiting/Wrasse.
Ragworm	— Bass/Coalfish/Cod/Conger Eel/Dab/ Dogfish/Flounder/Grey Mullet/Plaice/ Pollack/Pouting/Sole/Whiting/Wrasse.
Razorfish	— Bass/Coalfish/Cod/Dab/Dogfish/ Flounder/Plaice/Pollack/Pouting/Sole/ Wrasse.

Sandeel   — Bass/Coalfish/Cod/Conger Eel/Dab/
              Dogfish/Flounder/Mackerel/Plaice/
              Pollack/Pouting/Sole/Whiting/Wrasse.
Squid   — Bass/Coalfish/Cod/Conger Eel/Dab/
              Dogfish/Flounder/Pouting/Sole/
              Whiting/Wrasse.

Crabs

The common *shore crab* is best used for bait when the crab
has peeled its old shell, and temporarily become a "soft
back" crab. After a few days its soft back hardens into a new
shell. Hard-Back crabs cannot be fished successfully as bait.

Look for *peeler* crabs, about to shed their shells, and *soft-
backs*, in rock pools (see fig 61, on page 119) and under
stones in shallow estuary water from May/June onwards,
through summer.

The *hermit crab* (see fig 61, on page 119) finds an empty
shell in which to live, and can be found in rock pools. Break
the hermit's shell-home and remove the crab.

To kill shore crabs or hermit crabs wanted for bait, stab
between the eyes with a sharp knife. Snap off the claws.
Crabs can be spiked on a large hook whole, or cut into
sections, or the flesh stripped and fished separately.

Fish

Fresh *mackerel, herrings, sprats* and *pilchards* are rich in
natural oil and lay a strong scent trail for feeding fish to
follow.

Sandeels and *squid* often prove highly successful sea
fishing baits.

Catch fish for bait, or buy fresh fish from coastal
fishmongers, or at the quayside from commercial fishermen.

Frozen fresh fish is available from food stores, and
specialist tackle dealers.

Fish can be impaled on a large hook and fished whole, or
cut into chunks, fillets or strips.

Lure

Artificial lures include *spinners, spoons* and *pirks*. The many
different designs represent small fish (some designs more
obviously than others). Spinners and spoons are for

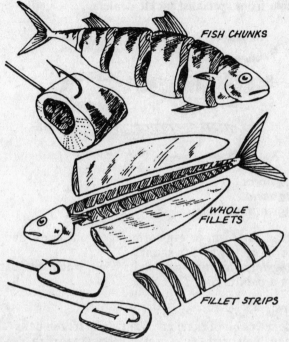

55. Fish strip and chunk baits.

spinning; pirks for jigging (see page 104).

Shellfish

Clams (sandgapers), *cockles* and *razorfish* live buried in sand and sand/mud (see fig 62, on page 122).

The *mussel* and *common limpet* (see fig 60, on page 116) cling to pier supports, rocks etc.

Gather shellfish at low tide. Carefully cut and scoop shellfish from their shells with a strong, thin-bladed knife. Fix on hook so the shellfish's tough, muscular "foot" is held secure on the hook's bend below the barbed hookpoint.

Worms

Lugworms and *ragworms* live in sand and sand/mud (see fig 62, on page 122). Subject to local bye-laws, they may be dug for bait. In some places, bait digging is illegal. However, a ready supply of lugworms and ragworms is conveniently available from specialist tackle dealers.

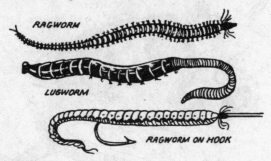

56. Ragworm.
   Lugworm.
   Ragworm on hook.

Thread lugworm or ragworm onto your hook, and slide the worm up the hook's shank.

A ragworm has tiny jaws in its head, which give careless fingers a painful nip. Take care.

Bait Tips
A wide selection of excellent, sea fishing frozen baits (crabs, herrings, lugworms, mackerel, mussels, razorfish, sandeels, sprats, squid etc.) is stocked by, or can be ordered from, your specialist tackle dealer.

Preserved baits are also marketed, though normally less effective than fresh or frozen baits.

Hook Tips
1. Keep hooks lip-piercing *sharp* – use an angler's special hook sharpening stone or tool.
2. Select the right size hook to suit your hookbait, and match the species and size of fish you're angling for. Small hook sizes 6 or 4 or 2 or 1 are suitable for most shore-feeding fish. Large hook sizes 1/0 or 2/0 or 3/0 or 4/0 are ideal where *Big* fish are anticipated.

Hook size guide   Fish
6 or 4 or 2 or 1 — Dab/Flounder/Mackerel/Grey
                    Mullet/Plaice/Pouting/Sole/
                    Whiting/Wrasse. Also young Coalfish/

Cod/Pollack.

1/0 or 2/0 or — Bass/Coalfish/Cod/Conger Eel/
3/0 or 4/0   Dogfish/Pollack. Also other species
of *Big* sea fish.

3. Slide your hook into the bait so that as much of the hook as possible is hidden from curious fish. Make certain the hook's sharp point sticks right through the bait, and is poised to penetrate the fish's lip the instant your line's pulled tight!

Activity
Keep a record of the baits you find most successful with particular species of sea fish. At the close of your sea fishing year, draw a chart comparing the effectiveness of baits fished. Your chart will help towards bigger and better catches in future years.

See my last year's sea bait chart below.

✱ = GOOD ✓ = EFFECTIVE ✗ = POOR	CRAB	LUGWORM	MACKEREL OR HERRING	RAGWORM	SANDEEL	SQUID	SPINNER SPOON PIRK ETC.
BASS	✱	✱	✓	✱	✱	✱	✓
CONGER EELS	✓	✗	✱	✗	✱	✱	
DABS	✓	✱	✗	✱	✱	✗	
DOGFISH	✱	✱	✱	✱	✱	✱	
FLOUNDERS	✱	✱	✱	✱	✱	✗	✓
SOLES	✓	✱	✓	✱	✓	✗	
WHITING	✱	✱	✱	✱	✱	✓	✓

57. Notebook: Sea bait chart.

22

ESTUARIES

Estuaries are sites where outflowing river freshwater mixes with incoming tidal saltwater. Estuaries often provide safe anchorage for boats, and many estuaries have developed into important centres of trade and commercial fishing.

Sea fish enter estuaries and cruise up river on rising high *(flood)* tides in search of food, and depart with the falling, low *(ebb)* tides. Some sea fish choose to stay between tides in estuary deep pools and channels.

FASCINATING FACT
The tidal power of rising and falling estuary water was first harnessed by *tide mills* in eleventh century England and Wales. Today, estuary tide power can be used to generate electricity.

Estuary fish: Bass, flounder, grey mullet, dab, plaice, conger eel, coalfish, freshwater eel; also sometimes cod and mackerel.
Right estuary methods include: Float fishing; driftlining; legering; paternostering; spinning; sink and draw (see page 29).
Great spots to fish
*Low tide deep pools and channels.
*The deep main channel on a rising tide.
*On, or slightly above, patches of mud or sand/mud colonised by ragworms or lugworms.
*Below drainage pipes and inflowing streams or rivulets of water.
*Close to sewage pipe outlets.
*Near weed-covered rocks, boulders and rocky channels.
*By jetty supports and boat mooring posts.
*Beside sunken hulls or submerged debris.
*Eddies of swirling water.
*Deep, slow water at the edge of turbulent currents.
*Quiet bays, channels or side-waters, where the main flow of water whisks food to waiting fish.

*Estuary mud flats which are flooded at high tide but exposed at low tide.
*Underneath bridges, and near bridge supports.

Estuary success hints

1. Inspect the exposed estuary at low tide; note great spots to fish as the tide rises, including the deep channels, gullies and bays that fill fast with water and accommodate the first wave of food-seeking sea fish.
2. Birds give us clues to spots where fish feed. The *common tern* is partial to sandeels, which also attract bass; *cormorants* signal the presence of flounders and freshwater eels.
3. Begin fishing as the tide rises; floods into the estuary and up river.
4. Estuary-feeding fish will seize freshwater baits (see Chapter 6).
5. Follow feeding shoals of sea fish at their pace up river. Aim to catch a few fish from the shoal at each popular feeding stop along route. Creep low; be quiet. Avoid sudden fish-scaring movements. If you lose contact with the shoal, remember they'll be back the same way on the outgoing *(ebb)* tide.
6. Groundbait (see page 102) scattered loose, or suspended in a fine-mesh bag draws fish to the spot you're fishing.
7. Expect good sport near the river mouth on the outflowing *(ebb)* tide; dislodged food is carried out to sea, followed keenly by returning sea fish.

Tackle + Tips

Estuary fishing can be enjoyed with light sea fishing tackle, or strong freshwater tackle. A rod of about 3.35m (11 feet) in length is ideal for general purpose estuary fishing; fixed-spool reel, and fishing line of round 4.53kg (10 lbs) breaking strain.

In addition to the main items of tackle recommended, you may find some of these extras worth buying or saving-up for.

● A long-handled adjustable (telescopic) large landing net is advisable to land hooked big estuary-feeding fish quietly and effortlessly.

● An angler's haversack stores essential tackle, straps comfortably over your shoulders, leaves you unencumbered by tackle bags or boxes, and free to pursue shoals of feasting fish on their steady progress up and down river.

Estuary nature trail

Look for the hardy and colourful flowering plants of estuary *salt marshes* – wide, flat expanses of mud and river-deposited silt covered by the highest tides: the regal purple of summer-flowering *sea lavender* and *sea aster* (see fig 63, on page 124); the pretty pink flowers of greater and lesser sea-spurrey, and sea milkwort.

58. Estuary.

1. Common Tern.
2. Grey Heron.
3. Shelduck.
4. Cormorant.
5. Sandling.

6. Curlew.
7. Redshank.
8. Oyster Catcher.
9. Little Ringed Plover.
10. Turnstone.

Shallow estuary waters are rich feeding grounds for many species of beautiful birds. Estuaries are a bird watcher's paradise. Take a small pair of binoculars or telescope, and enjoy your estuary fishing trip nature trail to the full!

23

HARBOURS, JETTIES AND PIERS

Harbour walls, jetties (projecting landing places) and piers are visited regularly by shoals of food-seeking fish.

Some deep water harbours have become all-year-round homes for sea fish who enjoy the sheltered water, and the dependable supply of discarded fish offal and food scraps tossed from commercial fishing boats, quayside traders, anglers and holiday-makers.

Large conger eels may live in pipes and cracks at the base of harbour walls!

Of special interest to hungry fish are the numerous crustaceans (crabs, shrimps etc.), molluscs (shellfish), marine worms, small fish and other creatures that live in plants, on rocks; pier and jetty supports, and in the ground beneath jetties, piers and harbour quaysides.

FASCINATING FACT

Seaweeds are nutritious plants. Many species of seaweed can be cleaned, cooked and served as delicious dishes!

Carragheen *(Chondrus crispus)* seaweed is an important ingredient in commercial ice-creams and toothpaste. Carragheen can be eaten on its own. To jelly: boil in water; leave to cool and set.

Laver *(Porphyra umbilicalis)* seaweed is prepared and eaten as tasty "laver cakes"; dulse *(Palmaria palmata)*, sea lettuce *(Ulva lactuca)* and sugar kelp or "sea belt" *(Laminaria saccharina)* seaweeds can be prepared and served as "bread", salad, stew or soup.

Fish caught from harbours, jetties and piers: Bass, coalfish, cod, conger eel, dab, dogfish, flounder, mackerel, grey mullet, plaice, pollack, pouting, sole, whiting, wrasse.

Right harbour, jetty and pier methods include: Float fishing; paternostering; legering; driftlining (where current carries line away from obstructions); spinning (from low-decked

59. Grey Mullet.

jetties, piers and low harbour walls).

Great spots to fish
*At the base of harbour walls; near posts, pillars; jetty and pier supports.
*The mouth of outlet pipes.
*Cracks, crevices and holes in harbour walls.
*Eddies of water whirling near harbour walls, or the supports of jetties or piers.
*Near weed growth on walls, posts and supports.
*Above sunken debris.
*Close to weed-covered rocks.
*On or above patches of sand or sand/mud.
*Seabed dips, hollows, gullies and holes.
*Areas of water where currents and swell churn the seabed, dislodging previously hidden food.
*Deep flows of water.

Harbour, jetty and pier success hints
1. Eye harbour walls, piers and jetties at low tide. Note places that will attract fish as the tide rises.
2. Watch for obstacles that may snag your line, and remember to avoid them when they're hidden from view by high tide water.
3. To fish from the best positions (which can become crowded) plan to arrive early, and beat late-comers to prime catches.
4. Dawn/early morning and late afternoon/evening usually give prize sport.

5. A rising *(flood)* tide produces the finest results, especially as the tide peaks at high tide level.

6. Groundbait (see page 102) scattered loose, or suspended in a fine-mesh bag attracts fish to the spot you're fishing.

7. *Legering* (see page 103) can bring good catches when water is at low tide level; *paternostering* (see page 103) is the best all-round harbour, jetty and pier method; *float fishing* (see page 101) is reliably effective on a rising *(flood)* tide; especially recommended as water approaches and settles at high tide level.

8. Reel-in hooked fish quickly. Don't permit them to dive around obstructions and snag your line. A sea angler's drop net (see page 100) may be required to land heavy fish from high harbour walls, jetties or piers.

Tackle + Tips
A strong rod of about 3.35m (11 feet) in length can be used for general purpose fishing from harbour wall, jetty or pier; fixed-spool reel, and fishing line of round 5.44kg (12 lbs) breaking strain.

In addition to the main items of tackle recommended, you may find some of these extras worth buying or saving-up for.

● An angler's sturdy tackle box holds all necessary bits and pieces, and provides a comfy seat for sit-down snacks.

● A sea angler's *drop net* (see page 100) is advisable for lifting big, heavy fish from the water without risk of fishing line breaking under the strain.

● A woolly hat that pulls over your ears and a pair of fingerless fishing mitts, prevent ear-ache and frozen hands in chill winds and icy weather.

Harbour, jetty and pier nature trail
At low tide look for exposed *barnacles* – when covered by water, they extend feather-like tentacles to catch food particles, and *mussels* (some contain small pearls!); also *common limpets* (most limpets are born male, and later change into females!).

Seaweeds can be green, brown or red. Green seaweeds grow mainly on the upper shore; browns and reds along the middle and lower shore, and reds into deeper water. Different colour seaweeds share parts of the shore, though red seaweeds may grow alone in places where little light normally penetrates.

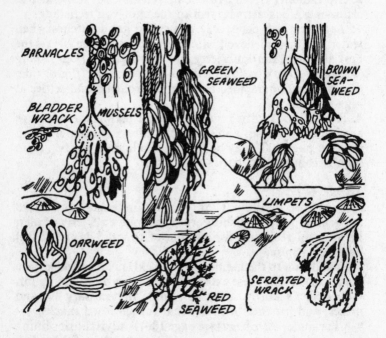

60. Pier supports on rocky shore.

24

ROCKY AND
SHINGLE SHORES

Rocky shores are nourishing feeding grounds for fish. Areas of sand or sand/mud between seabed rocks, supply fish with marine worms, shellfish etc; rocks provide places for fishes to hide, shelter from strong currents and ambush smaller fish. The craggy rock face is adhered to and populated by many edible creatures. Deep water directly below rocks offers marvellous angling opportunities.

Little grows or lives low on *shingle shores*. The wave-driven pebbles would crush the life from most plants or creatures. Fish feed over beds of sand or sand/mud, round submerged rocks, breakwaters etc.; wherever there is food and somewhere to hide.

FASCINATING FACT
The fierce Conger Eel *(Conger conger)* lurks round rocks, reefs and wrecks in all oceans and to depths greater than 3,000m! Mature male conger eels are often less than 1m in length; females can exceed 2m. All BIG (50kg +) congers are females who have not spawned. Some spawning female conger eels carry over 7½ million eggs. Conger eels spawn once, then die. Their average life-span is probably about 12 years.

Fish caught from rocky shores: Bass, coalfish, cod, conger eel, dogfish (bull huss), mackerel, pollack, pouting, sole (sand/mud between rocks), whiting, wrasse.

Sandy and muddy patches, or a rocky-rough bottom – beyond the pebbles of a barren *shingle shore,* attract species of fish that enjoy feeding on those types of seabed.

Right rocky and shingle shore methods include: Paternostering; float fishing; legering; spinning (in deep water); driftlining (tricky – tangles likely on rocky ground, but not inevitable).

Great spots to fish
*Deep water immediately beneath your rod tip, on rocky shores; also deep water close to your rod on steep sloping shores.
*Beside and just beyond breakwaters.
*In sheltered bays and backwaters, away from the crash and crush of powerful currents.
*Near masses of floating seaweed (float fishing best).
*On or above, patches of sand or sand/mud.
*Sandy/muddy channels between rocks.
*Whirling eddies, which trap and concentrate food for feeding fish.
*Close to weed and colonies of shellfish clinging to rocks, or breakwaters.
*At the entrance to caverns, hollows and crevices in rocks.
*Alongside undercuts which are scoured beneath safely solid and firm rock outcrops.

Rocky and shingle shore success hints
1. Check at low tide for great spots to fish.
2. A rising *(flood)* tide at dawn or dusk gives good sport.
3. Keep a tight line, and reel-in fish the instant hooked.
4. Steer hooked fish away from rocks, or your line will be snagged and snapped!
5. Fish feeding round rocks ride up the rock face as the tide rises. When float fishing, adjust float depth-settings accordingly.
6. Stay well back from the edge of rocks. Then you won't frighten fish, or fall in the sea!
7. Groundbait (see page 102) scattered loose, or suspended in a fine-mesh bag, leads fish to your hookbait.

Tackle + Tips
Beachcasting tackle and techniques (see Chapter 25) are ideal for shingle shores.

When fishing from rocks, you'll need a strong rod of about 3.35m (11 feet) in length; fixed-spool reel for general rock fishing, and fishing line of about 6.80kg (15 lbs) breaking strain.

In addition to the main items of tackle recommended, you may find some of these extras worth buying or saving-up for.

● An angler's haversack, or rucksack, stores tackle; fits snug on your back, and leaves hands free to help climb and clamber over rocks.

● A pair of properly laced, leather walking or climbing boots is very important, for scrambling safely across rocks.

● A sea angler's comfortable *flotation jacket* will keep you afloat if you drop in the sea. A flotation jacket is highly recommended – it may *save your life!*

● A sea angler's drop net (see page 100) helps land heavy fish.

Rocky and shingle shore nature trail
In summer, on the upper stretch of shingle/sand shores, look for the distinctive *yellow horned poppy* and *sea kale;* also *sea holly;* pink-flowering *sea bindweed,* and *sea beet* (see fig 63, on page 124).

Rock pools teem with life, and repay attentive study.

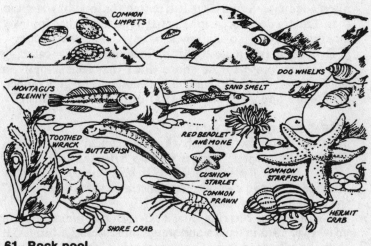

61. Rock pool.

Search carefully for shy water creatures, and plant-like animals. The aggressive *red beadlet* anemone (see "Rock pool" fig 61) stings small fish with its tentacles and swallows them whole. Beadlets also fight each other!

25

SAND AND MUDDY SHORES

Sand and sand/mud seabeds are favourite feeding places for many species of fish. Shellfish and worms shelter beneath the sand or sand/mud surface. Ocean swells, currents and waves dislodge creatures from the safety of their seabed retreats, making them easy prey for marauding shoals of fish.

The incoming *(flood)* tide carries feeding fish close inshore. Sometimes a long cast may be necessary to put your hookbait among feeding fish, but a cast of 25-35 metres is often adequate. Some large fish search for food in water less than 1 metre deep; occasionally fish grub the seabed for tasty pickings in water so shallow it barely covers their backs.

Driftlining (see page 101) is an ideal method for catching fish feeding close to the shore. Fish that feed happily in shallow water include: bass, dab, flounder, and grey mullet; also plaice and sole (best sport at dusk and after dark).

FASCINATING FACTS
Whales, dolphins and sharks swim near our shores. Periodically surprise visitors pop up from the sea!

The fierce Killer Whale *(Orcinus orca)* is highly intelligent, and in captivity demonstrates skills and "tricks" to the delight of audiences.

The harmless Basking Shark *(Cetorhinus maximus)* can grow over 13m in length and weigh more than 3.5 tonnes. It feeds on plankton (tiny floating organic life).

Giant Squid *(Architeuthis dux)* are the largest creatures with no backbone (invertebrates). Monster giant squid exceed 20m in length (including tentacles) and 2.25 tonnes in weight!

Fish caught from sandy and muddy shores: Bass, cod, dab, dogfish, flounder, mackerel, grey mullet, plaice, sole, whiting.

Right sandy and muddy shore methods include: Legering; paternostering; driftlining; also spinning in deep water off steep sloping shore.

Great spots to fish
*Patches of sand or sand/mud, particularly spots where colonies of lugworms, ragworms, or shellfish live.
*At the base of rocks or boulders, especially weed-covered and mollusc *(shellfish)*-encrusted rocks.
*On the sheltered side of breakwaters.
*Near masses of floating seaweed.
*Seabed dips, hollows and gullies.
*Areas of sand or sand/mud seabed disturbed by breaking waves and sucking currents.
*Tide-rips where 2 or more currents crash together to form whirlpools and white water.
*Troughs of water in front of, and/or behind, sandbanks.
*The quiet water of sheltered sandy or sand/mud bays.
*Where rivers or streams flow into the sea.
*Near outflow pipes (water, drainage, sewage etc.).

Activity
At low tide, explore the exposed sand or sand/mud seabed. Look for great spots to fish when the tide turns and flows back up the beach. Draw a map showing the angling "hotspots" for future reference.

Sandy and muddy shore success hints
1. Pick a peaceful place to fish, away from crowd noise.
2. Expect good sport the day after a major shore-fishing competition. Fishes come close inshore to mop up discarded baits.
3. Resist any temptation to leave your rod propped on a rod-rest while you laze on the beach. Hold the rod to be sure you don't miss bites, and lose fish!

4. Where, at low tide, you find seabed colonies of marine worms, shellfish etc., success is almost certain if you place your hookbait on that food-rich patch of seabed when the incoming tide floods the area. Use as bait a creature which fish would expect to find. Provided bait collecting is allowed, you can gather suitable live baits at low tide for use on the rising *(flood)* tide. Fig 62 shows the approximate depth at which live baits may be found.

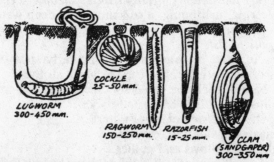

62. Looking for live "baits" in sand or sand/mud.

5. Fish feed close inshore for several days after a seabed-churning storm.

6. A cast to just beyond the third or fourth high-breaking wave often drops your hookbait in front of banqueting fish.

7. When high tide coincides with dawn, dusk or occurs after dark, anticipate good catches of fish close inshore on the incoming *(flood)* tide; particularly as the tide peaks at its high water level.

8. Birds give clues to help us catch fish. Where birds wheel and dive over shoals of small fish, we shall find large fish feeding. Common terns and gulls pin-point the position of mackerel and bass shoals.

Tackle + Tips
For long distance casting from the beach, a specially designed beach casting rod *(beachcaster)* is necessary. A beachcaster rod of about 3.35m (11 feet) in length is ideal for beginners; fixed-spool reel, and fishing line of round 13.60kg (30 lbs) breaking strain, to cast safely weights of up to 85g (3 oz).

In addition to the main items of tackle recommended, you may find some of these extras worth buying or saving-up for.
● A pair of lined, angler's knee-high boots, keep your feet dry and warm.
● A woolly hat, fishing mitts and thermal underwear, help you stay smiling in cold, miserable weather.
● A set of heavy duty waterproofs is essential to remain dry on rain and spray soaked beaches.
● A sea angler's rod rest gives you a chance *occasionally* to take a *brief* break from rod holding.
● A large capacity flask filled with hot soup warms and nourishes.

Sandy and muddy shore nature trail
Sandy seashore colourful plants to look for in summer (see fig 63) include the pink-flowering *sea bindweed;* yellow-green leaves and pea-like fruits of the *sea sandwort;* spiny-blue *sea holly;* purple *viper's bugloss;* also *sea beet* (related to all cultivated beets) and *marram grass,* which binds loose sand and stops sand drifting and being blown away.

Debris and food scraps washed ashore attract numerous animals and birds. Rabbits, hares, rats, mice, hedgehogs and foxes are regular seashore foragers.

Colonies of ragworms and pinky *catworms (Nephtys hombergi)* dwell below the surface of sand/mud at low tide, and emerge to hunt food on the incoming *(flood)* tide.

Lugworms eat the sand/mud washed into their U-shaped burrows (see fig 62), and live on the nourishment they filter from the sediment.

Beachcombing
Comb the beach for *treasure* deposited by the sea.
   Messages or treasure maps in bottles?
   Pirates' gold doubloons?
Maybe, but unlikely, although the treasure of pirate Captain William Kidd (1645-1701) has still to be found. Collectable personal "treasures" that excite our imagination, please the eye, and satisfy our collector's urge, are the treasure we seek.

Storms wash up many curiosities: timbers from old shipwrecks; knarled tree branches, and seeds that may have drifted across thousands of miles of oceans to reach us; beautiful and exotic sea shells and unfamiliar seaweeds.

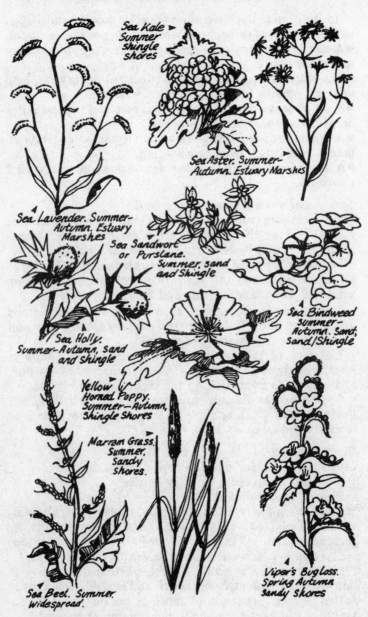

Sea Kale ▶ Summer shingle shores

Sea Aster. Summer—Autumn. Estuary Marshes

Sea Lavender. Summer—Autumn. Estuary Marshes

Sea Sandwort or Purslane. Summer, sand and Shingle

Sea Bindweed Summer—Autumn. Sand, Sand/Shingle

Sea Holly. Summer—Autumn, sand and Shingle

Yellow Horned Poppy. Summer—Autumn, Shingle Shores

Marram Grass. Summer, Sandy Shores.

Sea Beet. Summer. Widespread.

Viper's Bugloss. Spring Autumn Sandy Shores

63. Seashore plants.

Collect, clean, identify, label and display: eye-catching pebbles/stones and shells (some are valuable to collectors and as curios); interestingly shaped or home-sculpted driftwood. For special effect, bright pebbles and shells may be varnished, or part-painted and then varnished. Models can be crafted from glued shells.

Collect birds' feathers and mount them in a book, or on card. Identify each feather and describe the species of bird. Use surplus feathers to make floats (see page 20).

Photograph seashore flowers, seaweeds, and glorious seaside scenery.

And keep watch for Captain Kidd's treasure map!

Tight lines
I've enjoyed the fishing adventure we've shared in this book, and look foward to going fishing with you again soon. Till then, I wish you good health, great sport and tight lines!

INDEX

INDEX

Other lively fishing books by Ian Ball:
FRESHWATER FISHING PROPERLY EXPLAINED

Of the greatest value to beginner and experienced angler, this marvellous book is packed with facts, tips and hints to help you catch more and bigger fish.

SEA FISHING PROPERLY EXPLAINED

Here Ian explains all you need to know to make expert catches from beaches, rocks, estuary, pier, harbour wall or boat – don't let that big one get away!

THE SECRETS OF FLY-FISHING FOR TROUT

Ian Ball makes the essential fly-fishing skills simple and easy to understand.

Also available:
THE KNOT BOOK

Includes a chapter devoted to angling.

RIGHT WAY
PUBLISHING POLICY

HOW WE SELECT TITLES

RIGHT WAY consider carefully every deserving manuscript. Where an author is an authority on his subject but an inexperienced writer, we provide first-class editorial help. The standards we set make sure that every **RIGHT WAY** book is practical, easy to understand, concise, informative and delightful to read. Our specialist artists are skilled at creating simple illustrations which augment the text wherever necessary.

CONSISTENT QUALITY

At every reprint our books are updated where appropriate, giving our authors the opportunity to include new information.

FAST DELIVERY

We sell **RIGHT WAY** books to the best bookshops throughout the world. It may be that your bookseller has run out of stock of a particular title. If so, he can order more from us at any time – we have a fine reputation for "same day" despatch, and we supply any order, however small (even a single copy), to any bookseller who has an account with us. We prefer you to buy from your bookseller, as this reminds him of the strong underlying public demand for **RIGHT WAY** books. Readers who live in remote places, or who are housebound, or whose local bookseller is unco-operative, can order direct from us by post.

FREE

If you would like an up-to-date list of all **RIGHT WAY** titles currently available, please send a stamped self-addressed envelope to

ELLIOT RIGHT WAY BOOKS,
KINGSWOOD, SURREY, KT20 6TD, U.K.